ABOUT WOMEN

ABOUT WOMEN

{ *CONVERSATIONS BETWEEN*
A WRITER AND A PAINTER

LISA ALTHER
and
FRANÇOISE GILOT

NAN A. TALESE

Doubleday

New York   London   Toronto   Sydney   Auckland

Copyright © 2015 by Lisa Alther and Françoise Gilot

All rights reserved. Published in the United States by Nan A. Talese/
Doubleday, a division of Penguin Random House LLC, New York,
and distributed in Canada by Random House of Canada, a division of
Penguin Random House Ltd., Toronto.

www.nanatalese.com

DOUBLEDAY is a registered trademark of Penguin Random House LLC.
Nan A. Talese and the colophon are trademarks of
Penguin Random House LLC.

Book design by Maria Carella
Jacket design by Emily Mahon
Jacket art courtesy of Françoise Gilot

Library of Congress Cataloging-in-Publication Data
Alther, Lisa, author.
    About women : conversations between a writer and a painter /
Lisa Alther and Françoise Gilot.—First edition.
    pages cm
ISBN 978-0-385-53986-9 (hardcover)   ISBN 978-0-385-53987-6 (eBook)
1. Alther, Lisa. 2. Gilot, Françoise, 1921– 3. Authors, American—
20th century—Biography. 4. Women authors, American—
20th century—Biography. 5. Painters—France—Biography.
6. Women painters—France—Biography. I. Gilot, Françoise, 1921–
author. II. Title.
PS3551.L78Z46 2015
813'.54—dc23
[B]   2015003400

MANUFACTURED IN THE UNITED STATES OF AMERICA

10 9 8 7 6 5 4 3 2 1

First Edition

To the memory of
Virginia Woolf and Vanessa Bell,
whose mutually supportive creative relationship
inspired us both

Contents

ABOUT WOMEN

PREFACE

LISA ALTHER:

All through my school days, my drawings in art classes never looked the way I wanted them to. Later, once I discovered an aptitude for writing, I would probably have agreed with the philosopher Ludwig Wittgenstein when he said, "All I know is what I have words for."

Yet those who were able to pluck images out of thin air and re-create them on flat surfaces with paints and pencils continued to intrigue me. For twenty-some years, I was married to a painter, and I used to watch by the hour as his brushes and paints transformed canvases or watery sheets of paper into recognizable forms and figures. This process seemed almost magical to me.

At some point, though, I realized that what I did when I wrote was not so different: I would see in my head a shadowy scene involving strangers doing things I didn't understand. I would tell myself stories about these people until I could figure out who they were, and why they were behaving like that, and how their activities fitted into a larger plot that would eventually evolve into a short story or a novel. I used words instead of paints, but this process of extracting images from the ether was roughly the same.

After becoming friends with Françoise Gilot, I sometimes watched her construct monotypes on a lithographic press in SoHo or witnessed oil paintings in progress on her easel. One afternoon in her Paris studio, she gave me a watercolor lesson. I painted watercolors for several years afterward, discovering for myself a bit about how to translate the enigmatic figures lurking in my imagination into visual images on paper rather than into the words of a story.

One series of monotypes I watched Françoise compose in SoHo featured a strange mythological creature with a human body, large wings, and a beak-like nose. I named him Birdman and began to invent a story line for him, based on the successive monotypes as they emerged from the press. I wrote up this story and showed it to Françoise, who was astonished to discover her own kidnapped characters performing in my story, a story very different from the one she had been telling herself as she created the series. We later published this story in Holland, Denmark, and Germany under the title *Birdman and the Dancer*, using color plates of some of the monotypes as illustrations.

Françoise's French culture is very visual and produces lots of artists, fashion designers, and chefs. In contrast, my homeland, Appalachia, has a history of material deprivation. Since Appalachia's earliest settlement, its people have employed what was free and readily available to entertain themselves—their own voices. They sing, orate, preach, and tell jokes and stories. It's an aural culture, and an oral one. Growing up there, I was programmed to access the world via my sense of hearing.

But people are often drawn to what they lack, hoping thereby to complete themselves. My friendship with Françoise helped me to develop my eyes, overwhelmed for so long by my ears. The experience of sometimes viewing the world through her eyes and her art work opened up for me an alternate pathway for apprehending reality, one that complements and enriches my own.

FRANÇOISE GILOT:
Even for the most dedicated artists in each and every mode of expression, the creative process is, and remains, mysterious. It's as if from the start, the friendship that developed between Lisa Alther, an American novelist, and myself, a painter originally from France, had a lot to do with a mutual curiosity about what sets off and nurtures the artistic imagination. Each, facing the other, reflected to the infinite the combination of shapes and colors, as in parallel mirrors. From this confrontation, our hope was that unexpected aspects of forms and meaning could and would become manifest.

It is a well-known fact that women are often gifted *raconteuses*. Retelling legends or personal remembrances, they transmit the power of speech to the next generation. Therefore, it's quite natural that we selected dialogues as the easiest means for communicating the enthusiasm necessary to promote the flight of the imagination in both writing and painting. It is often thanks to anecdotes relating unusual information that we succeed in taming important ideas and unexpected phenomena.

Even though my paintings are not illustrative, I spend much of my time telling myself stories, which often are at the origin of my drawings or canvases. In 1953, for example, I started to think about two friends, one of whom read to the other a poem she had composed, relating to a mysterious woman named Zulma. Her name started at the end of the alphabet (with a Z) and ended at its beginning (with an *a*), composed of five letters, like the fingers on a human hand. The name had come to me from Balzac on account of his real or imaginary friend Zulma Carraud. The Zulma story provoked me and helped me to create most of my paintings and drawings during that year. It also helped me to remain balanced, even though I was going through the difficult process of ending my ten-year relationship with Pablo Picasso, taking my children Claude and Paloma, aged six and four, respectively, back to Paris from Vallauris to start school.

All this has receded into the past as events followed events and many changes occurred through time. Yet this poetic hope endured—for a garden where, beyond love's catastrophes, there exists a possibility of more peaceful relationships in which grace replaces greed and peace replaces war.

In my mind, I can still hear our two voices—one more clear, flying high above life's events, lyrical, and the other more mezzo, lead colored, accessible to fits of melancholy—the two voices a testimony to friendship.

The Story of Zulma, Françoise Gilot, 1953,
crayons and pencil, 20" x 26"

I. THE WAR ROOM

LA: Although we were born of different generations an ocean apart, both our childhoods were impacted by war—yours by World Wars I and II, and mine by World War II, the Cold War, Korea, and Vietnam. We read a lot about the effect of war on the combatants but not that much about its effect on civilians. Can you say something about how war affected you as a child?

FG: My maternal grandmother had five children, two of whom died when they were quite young, leaving two sons and my mother, the youngest. The child my grandmother loved best was named André. He was wounded at the front and died on November 1, 1918, from a shrapnel wound to the liver. The armistice occurred on November 11, 1918. Just when my grandmother thought that her two sons had escaped the war, she learned the tragic news. André was only twenty-three years old. She had had a special relationship with him, so for her it was as if life ended right then and there.

On the third floor of her home in Neuilly, there was a small room where her sons, my uncles, both of them officers, had collected all sorts of paraphernalia from the different phases of the war. Many photographs were pinned to the walls, as well as war maps with little flags on pins for the various events. This room was left as it had been when André died. On the walls, one could see all these black-and-white photographs, some taken from the sky, of destroyed villages and cathedrals and bridges, charred forests, trenches. It was a room entirely full of destruction.

LA: Why did your uncles do this?

FG: I think they were so involved in the fight that destruction had grown inside them. They had had to withstand so much horror, and perhaps it was a catharsis to objectify their feelings on the walls of that room.

Years later, when I entered it for the first time, it felt very strange. I was five years old. It was quite frightening. There were also some half-exploded bombshells that looked like dark and ghostly flowers. My grandmother called that room the War Room. I thought it was the Death Room.

My mother and grandmother installed a seamstress there with a sewing machine. They were planning dresses for me, both in velvet. My mother's design was to be made of royal blue velvet in a cut called princess, with a little bodice to the waist and a skirt that was corolla-shaped, like a flower.

Whereas my grandmother's dress design was modern, Art Deco, straight, and very short, with assorted bloomers since it was so short that it showed my bottom. It was turquoise blue because she felt that was the color that suited me best. From her samples of turquoises, I had selected the one I wanted, as I also had for my mother's royal blue.

I was intrigued and pleased to touch the samples of

Aerial photograph from the War Room showing
bombed-out ruins of the Château de Brimont in the
upper-left quadrant (1917).

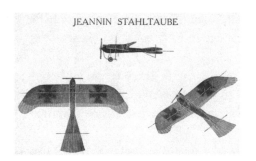

JEANNIN STAHLTAUBE

A diagram of a World War I German airplane taken
from *Silhouettes d'avions,* a booklet owned by Françoise's
uncle, an artillery officer. The booklet identified aircraft
by nationality to help gunners target correctly.

velvet. I chose the material that felt the softest. Then they showed me both pieces of fabric, and I watched the transformations leading from the material to the finished dresses. Maybe it's even more striking to me in retrospect, because, as a painter, I also give things shape and color. They had drawn models, and the seamstress cut the material and assembled the parts to look like the sketches. It was the first time I had any inkling of that kind of transformation. Paradoxically, this lovely and so feminine process was taking place in that strange room.

LA: Did it have photos of dead people also?

FG: No, just those photographs of ravaged landscapes and all the destruction.

LA: Did you have any idea what it meant?

FG: Yes, the adults were often talking about the Great War. Everybody was still fixated on it, maybe because of so many losses and hardships. The war had ended only in November 1918. I was five in 1927, so these events were not so far away.

Yet people were also living in the present, enthused over Josephine Baker and fast cars. The war, which concerned death, provided, by contrast, a reference point for life.

To me, it was all very mysterious and morbid. That seamstress, who could have worked in any other room, had been set up precisely there, with the sewing machine and a life-sized dummy (similar to those in Giorgio de Chirico's paintings). The scene reminded me of the story of the sleeping princess who, when she goes up to the tower (the abode of an old crone who is in fact a bad witch in disguise), pricks herself with the tip of a spindle. She goes to sleep for a hundred years, along with everyone else in the castle.

So for me, the fact that the seamstress was in that room with a needle in hand was dangerous. I hesitated between interest in what was going on—that transformation of a piece of cloth into a dress—and terror of a more drastic metamorphosis. The dress my mother had designed, instead of having simply a hem at the bottom, was scalloped. There were teeth, like arcs of circles, and there were also small arcs to end the little sleeves. I thought that was clever and unusual, and maybe also a magical protection.

The name of that seamstress was Adèle, and she was beautiful in a dark, classical way. I always liked the letter A, maybe because it's the first letter of the alphabet. I preferred a woman's name to start with an A or end with one. I thought that Adèle was a strange name. I liked the sound of the A and the d, but not the "èle."

On top of it all, there was a silly song in French that had a leitmotif: "Car elle est morte Adèle, Adèle ma bien aimée." And in French "morte Adèle" is heard as "mortadelle," the name for an Italian sausage. So it meant, "She's dead, Adèle my beloved," but it also meant that she was an Italian sausage. And since she was in the War Room with all its reminders of death, I just couldn't think of anything other than that stupid song.

I guess that, unconsciously, my mother and grandmother wanted to transcend the war with something specifically soft and feminine. They were not conscious of it themselves, for sure, but I suspect that's why they selected that sad room in which to establish the seamstress.

LA: The good witches, sewing their spells. What an image! My very first memory is from when my father came back from World War II. He was wearing his olive army jacket. I must have been about three. I think we were at a cabin in Tennessee in which his parents lived briefly after they gave us their house. I remember him looming over me, backlit by a lightbulb in the ceiling, and I remember the floor. It was linoleum, black-and-white squares. And I remember a gold-and-brown snake, a copperhead, I now realize, slithering across those black-and-white squares.

FG: A snake, an actual snake?

LA: Yes, a real snake. It had gotten into the kitchen somehow. My grandfather chased it out the back door and chopped its head off with a shovel.

I felt a kind of horror about the whole situation. My mother and I must have been very close while my father was gone. I was a baby, and she was probably lonely and unhappy, left alone to cope with my two-year-old brother, John, and me. But now my father was back.

FG: Oh, that's quite a symbolic memory. The living paradise . . .

LA: Paradise lost. He was back, and the next thing I knew, my second brother, Bill, had been born.

FG: Was your crib in your mother's room until then?

LA: I'm not sure. When I was ten days old, my father went to boot camp in Pennsylvania, leaving my mother and older brother, John, and me at his parents' house. He was assigned to an army base in Cheyenne, Wyoming, so we followed him out there from Tennessee in our car. My mother drove thirty-five miles per hour to spare the tires and save gas, so it must have taken us many days to get there.

John sat in the front seat beside my mother. She said he talked nonstop, and she focused on him because she didn't want him to feel replaced by the new baby (me) or upset by his father's disappearance. Later on, when I started talking, she said my first complete sentence was "Mommy, please make John stop talking all the time."

My car seat was an orange crate on the floor of the backseat. It must have been very unsettling for a new baby, all alone on that shadowy floor, the car swaying, not knowing where I was or where my mother was or what was happening. The seat back was very high and padded, and my mother couldn't really hear me over John's chatter and the music on the radio and the roar of the engine and the hum of the tires on the road. So I was unable to signal when I was wet or hungry or frightened. I was fed and changed whenever we stopped for gas or for meals.

Once we reached Wyoming, my father was sent to Abilene, Texas, and we followed along in the car. I've seen some photos from Abilene, including one of my parents and my brother taken on Thanksgiving Day, but I don't appear in any of them. It makes me wonder if they'd forgotten me on the back floor of the car.

In Abilene, my father, who was a doctor, was put on a troop train with the window shades closed. It was a secret mission, and we weren't told where he was going.

He ended up in England, after a voyage across the North Atlantic on a troopship that was swarmed several times by German submarines. He talked of his horror at watching oil slicks and body parts and debris from the destroyed subs rise to the surface of the ocean. During one attack, he had to perform an emergency appendectomy using dinner forks as retractors because someone had for-

Car in which Lisa, her mother, and her brother
drove cross-country, parked outside their apartment
in Abilene, Texas (autumn of 1944).

Lisa (after three months in her orange crate), her father, John Shelton Reed, on the eve of his departure for World War II in Europe, and her brother John (November 15, 1944).

gotten to send along any surgical instruments. He received some kind of medal for this feat. One of his main jobs was to give shots of penicillin to the several hundred soldiers with syphilis on board.

Meanwhile, my mother and John and I drove back to my grandparents' in Tennessee. And eventually we drove to my mother's home in upstate New York, where we lived in a cottage on a lake with two of my aunts and their children. Their husbands were also away fighting in the war.

I traveled forty-two hundred miles in my orange crate during my first ten months, and I lived in seven different places by the time I was two and a half, to say nothing of all the motels we stopped at during our travels. It's no wonder I became a bit of a nomad once I grew up.

I'm told I woke up crying many nights during this upheaval, at about 3:00 a.m. My poor mother would walk me to calm me down. But when she tried to put me back in my crib, I'd start crying again and wake up John, so she sometimes brought me back into bed with her. I can imagine that having been alone all day in the orange crate, I must have needed some human contact—too bad for me that it was given by an exhausted and annoyed mother and only to shut me up.

No doubt my happy hours in my mother's bed ended abruptly when my father came back. He used to complain that I was a show-off, making cute faces at neighboring tables when we went out to dinner and rolling down the lawns outside restaurants in my smocked dress. But I was probably just trying to retrieve some of the attention I'd lost upon his return and the birth of my baby brother.

I hate to say it, but the tragedy for many babies born during wars was not that their fathers went away but rather that they came back! We never bonded with our fathers as infants, or they with us, because they weren't around.

Cottage on Conesus Lake in western New York State in which Lisa, her mother, and brother lived in 1945 while her father was in Europe for World War II.

After my parents' deaths, I read in my mother's day-book from the year of my father's return that he hit me in the head with a golf club. She gives no details, and it was never mentioned later on. I assume it was an accident, but I wish I knew for sure.

I must have complained a lot that I wasn't a boy because I remember my mother always saying to me, "Yes, but you're our only little girl." What I minded most was that unlike my brothers I couldn't pee standing up. Despite this handicap, I did believe I was a boy for several years. In the summer, I wore only shorts, no shirt, like my brothers. But when I was about six, the other kids started making fun of me, so I began wearing shirts. That same year, I started school and discovered I couldn't wear jeans as my older brother did but instead had to wear dresses. This was a horrible shock.

When my father came home from working at the hospital, whoever was sitting in his chair had to move. My mother, who had been working just as hard as he all day, jumped up and began to serve him. Sometimes he went straight to bed with a headache, and she brought him a meal on a tray. But if she were sick, he was always at work. Marriage didn't look like a fair deal to me.

FG: It seemed to me also that men were much more privileged in life than women. I had a tendency to say, "Yes, what a pity I'm not a boy."

At the same time, my grandmother was telling me, "A woman is in no way inferior to a man, only different."

I just couldn't make sense of all that. Why should you think it was so impressive to be a woman when obviously women got the short end of the stick? All their preaching about feminism fell on deaf ears at that time.

Also, they were always talking about the Virgin Mary.

But I wasn't interested in the Virgin Mary in the least. It's convenient because in Catholicism monotheism is mitigated. You can choose to be devoted to the aspect that you prefer. I didn't feel all that much enthusiasm for God the Father, and Christ was an ascetic, a little bit alien to my nature. The Holy Ghost was the only one of the Trinity I was interested in. The spirit of creation was my thing. I could understand it. I thought it was marvelous.

When we entered a church, my mother and grandmother would always go to the left to pray at the altar of the Virgin Mary. But I always went as close as I could to the center, which is interesting because that's been my inclination in many matters. My father didn't go to church at all.

LA: I suppose a way for pious, fairly conventional women to express a kind of independence is to worship through the Virgin Mary rather than through Jesus.

FG: Absolutely. There was only one cross in my grandmother's house, for when somebody died, but it was not out at ordinary times. There were some religious images in the bedrooms—angels, saints, the Madonna, even Christ as a child, looking in good health. But there was no cross because they said it brings bad luck! They used to say, "If you want to meditate on a crucifix, go to church."

LA: So your mother and grandmother were always saying that women were equal to men, but you could see that it wasn't true?

FG: Well, they were always trying to find heroines for me, role models that I would accept. I was told that during the Second Empire (before 1870) my great-grandmother

Madame Renoult had refused to follow her husband, an engineer, to Egypt, where he joined Mr. de Lesseps for the piercing of the Suez Canal. Instead, she went back with her young son to her natal city of Brioude in Auvergne. Once there, she joined a "George Sand Atelier" where women met once a week to create good works to benefit women in need and to theorize about women's role in the world. Apparently, she was deeply convinced of the importance of George Sand's message, since she later convinced not only her daughter-in-law but also her granddaughter, my mother. Later in life, my mother often went to Nohant, George Sand's home, as a kind of pilgrimage.

But I couldn't understand why, since my grandmother was very good at business and my mother was doing applied arts, it didn't bring them into the light. So when they said it was the same to be a man or a woman, I was not quite convinced. I felt men had made the whole world their oyster. My grandmother was a feminist, but as a child I was not a feminist. I became a feminist later on when I understood what it meant.

Apart from me, my maternal grandparents had no other grandchild. My uncle Lucien was not married, and my mother had no other children. I was somehow supposed to be carrying on the line. They took great care about the way I was dressed, almost like a flower, and about my education, because I was the only future they had.

It was hard for me to fathom being told that I was intelligent like my uncle André, and that I was to replace for my grandmother and mother the favorite son, the favorite brother. That's one of the reasons I was brought up a bit like a boy. He was an engineer with a diploma from a school equivalent to MIT, and he was very courageous. Since he died when he was twenty-three, he hadn't had time to do anything wrong, so they idealized him. I did not think I could ever emulate this mythical being.

My father also wanted me to be a son—a daredevil, climbing trees, sailing with him—because he didn't have another child. But he also wanted me as his intellectual companion. When I was about ten and he saw that I was clever, he decided I should be like a son, rational and masculine.

At the same time, they were also teaching me how to be a girl. As a matter of fact, I was supposed to be a boy during the week and a girl on Sundays and holidays. So I had to be the young man they had lost, the son my father hadn't had, and also the young girl I really was. It was hard; it was really hard!

I'm androgynous because I was made that way. I don't think I ever had a choice. In order to satisfy all those people, I had to be both. I don't think it was conscious on their part. When you see things in retrospect, it seems very clear. But when things are actually happening, they aren't that clear.

Also, in that generation people weren't very aware of their unconscious motives. If it had been me, I'd have asked myself why I was doing that. But they weren't given to such self-analysis. They started by assuming that they were always right.

LA: But in the long run, being expected to be both a boy and a girl was probably very much to your advantage, because you developed the strengths of both sides of yourself.

FG: In retrospect perhaps, but at the time it was extremely painful and confusing. I didn't know if I was a boy or a girl.

Also, I was born left-handed, and I was required to change hands when I was three. I became cross-eyed and started to stammer. When you change hands, you're a mess for a year.

I don't think the adults realized what sort of effort they were asking of me. I understood only later that I went through experiences that were fairly difficult. To come to know who you are, little by little, through all that imbroglio is a challenge.

LA: You got too much attention from people trying to shape you.

FG: I was everyone's guinea pig. If I had been less strong, I'd have been destroyed. Part of me was quite advanced, but part of me was very reluctant.

As a child, I had a terrible dream that I was running in front of a train about to overtake me, and I had to run faster than the train. For some reason, I couldn't get off the tracks. In another version of the same dream, I was running behind the train, trying to catch up!

I didn't see any use for the feminine side that was developed in me until I was fifteen. All of a sudden I looked at myself in the mirror. Before that, I didn't pay too much attention. I just adopted that persona when I needed it. But at fifteen, I could see what I could really do with it, and it became interesting.

LA: What you were trained to be as a woman in France was less cloying than what being a woman can involve in the United States. For me, to be a woman meant to run a household and have babies and take care of a husband. I went to cooking classes and sewing classes and babysitting classes and charm school, where we were taught how to stand and walk and put on makeup. But for you, being a woman meant being a femme fatale.

FG: I was not taught to cook at all. I was not taught about babies. I had no brothers or sisters. But I *was* taught that I should become a professional woman.

LA: When I went to Wellesley College, I was also taught that a woman needed a skill with which she could support herself. But when I was a child, womanhood looked like slavery to me.

FG: For me, it looked strange and distant, and performing the part was a comedy. Of course, I was proud of being able to come to my mother's tea parties and make my little curtsy and behave appropriately, but reality was not there. At fifteen, however, all of a sudden the boys were eager to dance with me.

LA: So it was a source of power, female power?

FG: Exactly. That is when I realized that, after all, it involved power and status, so I adopted that side of myself. I became an actress; I identified with the part.

For me, a good example of that female power in action is the story of my maternal grandmother's visit to her sons at the front during World War I. She knew their general, so she put on an elaborate hat with ostrich feathers and hired a taxi to drive her from Paris to the headquarters. Using all her charm, she asked the general to give her a pass to go see her sons.

He said, "But, dear madame, they are on the front line. They're in the trenches. Of course you can't see them."

"If it's good enough for my sons," she replied grandly, "it's good enough for me."

Finally, he gave in, and she made the terrified taxi driver take her to the front line. The people who were the most annoyed were her sons. They were the only ones whose mother came to see them in the trenches to find out how they were doing and to bring them chocolates.

LA: Romain Gary in *Promise at Dawn* described himself during World War II in his leather aviator jacket, surrounded by his comrades, when his mother arrived to check up on him. He received letters from her throughout the war, only to discover afterward that she had died, leaving packets of letters for a friend to mail to him regularly so that he wouldn't learn of her death and become demoralized.

FG: Yes, and he couldn't understand why her letters were a bit irrelevant to what he had written her!

Some people think Frenchwomen were unconcerned by what was going on during World War II because they remained as elegant as they could. That was the period when they wore the most extravagant hats. Since there were no cars, everyone had to travel in the subway. So in the evening you saw those marvelous hats, and the Germans couldn't comprehend why Frenchwomen would be so frivolous as to think about something like that at that time.

In fact, it was because the Germans had forbidden the French to use fabric for frivolous purposes that we found old things in the attic and used them to make hats—just to annoy the Germans and to make it clear to them that French people were not down on their knees. It was to illustrate to them that Paris was the city of fashion and that whatever they did to us in the way of repression, we were still the city of fashion, whether they liked it or not.

A woman named Madame Bianchini belonged to a famous family, part French and part Italian, who created the most beautiful printed silk fabric for haute couture. During the war, she made hats with birds on them, as a way to express her antagonism and independence.

Normally, you need felt to make a hat, but we used cardboard to make the armature, which was then covered with fabric. We weren't allowed to buy new fabric, but many had plenty of old fabrics they could transform. My grandmother Gilot's grandmother had been in fashion and up in her attic were stunning samples of silk velvet, which I sewed together to make the most beautiful bonnet you can think of. I called it my Rembrandt bonnet, a huge one like you see in some paintings by Rembrandt.

LA: Madame Bianchini in her memoirs mentions making dresses of old drapes, like Scarlett O'Hara in *Gone with the Wind* during the Civil War. The comedian Carol Burnett did a parody of that scene, descending a spiral staircase in a gown made of curtains, with the curtain rod still inserted, balanced on her shoulders.

FG: I also went to the flea market to buy inexpensive, ugly paintings so I could paint on the other side, since fresh canvases were not available at any price. At the same time, I'd buy theater costumes, adapting them to my purposes.

LA: If the Nazis were basically sadists, then by destroying everything on which you prided yourselves, they hoped to demoralize you from within. But it seems that many French just continued to do what they'd always done and refused to cooperate.

Françoise's parents' house in Neuilly, where she lived with her own children and which she owned until 1986.

FG: In Paris, you had to take the subway whether you liked it or not. Either that or a bicycle. You might have a car in your garage, but if you had gas for it, it meant you were in cahoots with the Germans. My father, as the head of an industry, was entitled to gasoline, but he never used his car during the entire war, because he didn't want to accept gasoline from the Germans.

At that time, there was one car in the center of each metro train that required a more expensive ticket. Only German officers could go into first class, and the French-women wearing those marvelous hats ignored them as though they didn't exist. The Frenchmen who weren't with de Gaulle or in jail would accompany us, and we all tried to look rather aloof. I believe it annoyed them a lot. That was one of the few ways we could retaliate, qualitatively if not in kind.

During the war, I sometimes went by train to Languedoc with a hidden letter for someone in the Resistance, and I would dress in my best clothes and ride in first class. Nobody, German or otherwise, bothered me because my attire was such that no one thought to address me.

In a different vein, bicycling through Paris, as I did all the time, I decided to use my trips to manifest my opinions. So I dressed in blue, red, and white, to be a sort of banner on wheels. The jacket was vermilion red, the trousers to the knees royal blue, the sweater and stockings pure white wool or cotton. I liked it best when I was riding on the Place de la Concorde, just across from the huge Nazi flags of black, red, and white covering several seventeenth-century buildings. I must say, no one ever stopped me!

LA: Returning to the aftermath of World War I, I think you said there was a large room next door to the War Room at your grandmother's house that became your playroom?

Bicyclists riding beneath Nazi flags on the Place de la Concorde in Paris during the German occupation.

FG: Yes, it had been my mother's studio before she married, where she practiced applied arts and painted watercolors. When I was eight, my mother and grandmother decided it would become my playroom. As an only child, I usually played there alone, except for my cocker spaniel, Peluche. I called her Dame Peluche because she was very dignified.

I had a well-equipped puppet theater with a curtain and backdrop and the usual French puppets—Guignol, la mère Michel, Colombine, et cetera. One is the bad boy, another the disagreeable old lady, another a rather pretty girl. Polichinelle is hunchbacked in both the back and the front, and he brings in the unusual or unexpected, and he also philosophizes. All those characters are quite archetypal.

LA: Like the ones you see in the street theaters who are always beating each other over the head?

FG: Yes, like the puppet theaters in the Champs-Élysées and in the Jardin du Luxembourg. These were a very traditional type of puppet that existed mostly in Paris, and I think the characters are more or less from the Italian commedia dell'arte. But I'm not sure.

For the benefit of my dog, I'd invent plays in which those puppets were doing something appropriate to their persona. It was completely obvious that the dog didn't get much out of it, but it never occurred to me to ask my grandmother to come watch. While busy inventing my performance and manipulating the puppets and speaking with different voices, I was entirely enthusiastic and involved, and the lack of an audience didn't occur to me.

The dog sat there in an armchair and watched. To me, the dog was a person. I made my stuffed dog Fricket attend as well. So the real dog and the fake dog sitting side by side were my public. A few times, I asked the cook as well, but she would watch for five minutes and find a reason to leave.

I was too busy to be lonely. I also had a marvelous circus with articulated puppets made of painted wood with beautiful costumes in satin. They could do somersaults, et cetera, and I used some of them for my plays.

Many times I wreaked havoc in my playroom. All those scraps left over from the seamstress were put in a basket for me. I had a mania for cut, cut, cutting them with my scissors into bits and pieces. I found so much pleasure cutting into colored fabrics.

LA: A young Matisse.

FG: But I wasn't doing anything except cutting them into tiny bits. When I started to cut, a madness would engulf me. I think it was a postponed reaction to all the destruction portrayed in the War Room. My grandmother and the seamstress called me *la coupe-hacheuse*—the madwoman who cuts! They pretended that once I started, everyone had to go away until everything was cut into tiny shreds.

LA: *Hacheuse.* That's what you call hamburger, isn't it?

FG: Yes, I was making hamburger of the fabric! My grandmother, my mother, and the seamstress were also cutting, but they were cutting to transform a rectangle of fabric into a shape. To a child, this was extremely mysterious, and I could not get the hang of it. So by cutting randomly, I thought I would get somewhere.

In the beginning, maybe I had an idea of what I wanted, but since it never turned out my way, I just kept cutting, until the cutting itself became the goal. My grandmother thought it was a bizarre psychological aspect in me. She and the cook would discuss whether or not I was destructive.

LA: Maybe it was your version of the *furia francese*—the frenzy French soldiers used to go into on medieval battle-fields. It terrified the Italians.

FG: That *furia* lasted until I was twelve. I was very high-strung. When I wanted to paint a watercolor, I had to be so cool that I could not do anything interesting. If I let myself go, I would get into such a high-wire mood that I would become completely insane and tear the paper apart.

Very often for a painter, a moment comes when things go sour, and I had to train myself to summon the energy not to destroy the piece and to oblige myself to continue. That is what really makes you an artist. The passion you need to create can become its own negation. There's a fantastic sentence by Saint Augustine that goes something like: *En faisant ce qu'il voulait, il arrivait où il ne voulait pas.* By doing what he wanted, he arrived where he didn't want to be.

Things just didn't come out the way I had planned. Then I got into a frenzy because I thought I had taken all the right steps to achieve what I wished. I would lock the door and tear the thing apart and roll on the floor on top of it. Not screaming, because I didn't want to make noise. It was almost like a fit of epilepsy. It was as though creativity were a horse I could not master.

Strangely enough, I started to ride horses when I was ten, and it took me until age twelve to begin to work well with a horse, and with myself, and with the two of us together making one. Dealing with a horse, such a power-ful animal, physically much stronger than myself, probably helped me deal with myself.

LA: I had much more freedom to run wild. We built tree houses and went on daylong hikes through the woods. When we rode horses at our farm, it was often bareback. We had real rifles with which we shot tin cans off rock ledges and mistletoe out of the tops of oak trees. But that's the difference between urban and rural childhoods. We had very little supervision. Or rather, as the older sister, I was the supervisor, God help my younger brothers! The adults didn't want to mold us; they just wanted us out of the house and out of their hair.

FG: Maybe my rages of destruction were because I was growing up in a kind of hothouse. My puppets might have been a sublimation of a divided personality.

For the first time, when I was twelve, I cut fabric with which I was able to make something that really looked the way I wanted it to. And I started to be able to make water-colors that looked a bit the way I wanted them to as well. So at that point, I asked my grandmother's maid to teach me how to use the sewing machine.

LA: I think it must be part of the creative process. You have to arouse a certain amount of energy or passion in order to want to create something. In my case, I'd work on something, and once the workday was over, I'd become extremely depressed at seeing how far it was from what I'd envisioned. My tendency would be to want to destroy it and/or kill myself.

But with a novel or a short story, it might be months or years before you're finished. For me, so much of learn-

Lisa climbing a tree at twenty months.

The 1820 log cabin on Lisa's family's farm in Jonesborough, Tennessee, where they spent weekends and summers.

ing to write has been learning to ignore that destructive impulse that always comes after the exhilaration of the creative impulse. Now I know that it's just part of my psychic mechanism. I have the incredible satisfaction of doing the work, and then there's a rebound brought on by exhaustion. I've had to train myself to ignore that and to assure myself, "This despair isn't real, it's just the price you have to pay, it will pass, tomorrow you'll feel the enthusiasm again." It's like a mild case of manic depression.

FG: When I became more advanced, I experienced that, too. When you create, you always think it's good. Then you look at it, and you're displeased.

But I'm talking about not even being able to get to first base. When I was a child, the passion was so strong, and it had to burn itself out. I associate it with that playroom, my mother's former studio, next door to the famous War Room. When I was sixteen, I changed that playroom into my first studio. I redid the interior decoration.

I was in a philosophy class, and my friends would come to discuss philosophy. I wasn't at that point entirely decided on what I would become, and philosophy was one possibility.

LA: Your mother no longer painted?

FG: Not for a long time. She had forsaken her first vocation.

LA: So she went from the studio to the sewing room—the opposite direction from your trajectory.

FG: My mother's decoration was somewhat Chinese— beautiful heavy cotton drapes with an abstract pattern in tones of gray, yellow ocher, and saffron yellow. It was nice, but I had seen it enough.

When I was sixteen, I decided to put my imprint on that room, so for the window curtains I bought blue-and-white chintz. One armchair was the same color, and the other was tea rose in heavy satin. I had an eighteenth-century secretary, which my uncle gave me. There were lots of books around. It was a place to write as well as to paint.

My taste was British influenced. At that time, I adored Virginia Woolf and all the British writers. I had a deep case of Anglomania, and I had spent several summers near Portsmouth learning English with a British family I greatly loved and admired.

I discovered Virginia Woolf in philosophy class at the age of sixteen. The other girls in my class were also quite intellectual, so we had incredible discussions after hours, often in my studio. That was in 1938–39. Some British friends who lived in Paris also came there. I conducted a bit of a salon. Since I was studying so hard, I didn't have much time then for painting.

Then came World War II, which began in September 1939. That period was called *la drôle de guerre* because, until the Germans invaded Norway, nothing much happened for a few months. I was in my first year in law school, partly in Paris and partly in Rennes in Brittany, because my father thought there would be bombing raids on Paris. Then came the armistice, which was disastrous.

In 1940 on the eleventh of November, which was the anniversary of the armistice of 1918, many students decided to go put some flowers on the grave of the unknown soldier at the Arc de Triomphe. Even though it wasn't organized, many students in Paris had the same idea. Some German soldiers were pushed around. Some students were put in jail and kept there. Many managed to escape. Although I fled, I didn't get away in time, so some policemen took down my name and address.

A few days later, I was summoned to the French police office in Neuilly, where I was informed that I was on a list of hostages. For every German soldier killed in a given area in the future, fifty students would be executed in reprisal. I don't know exactly why they picked me. It might have been because my father wouldn't collaborate and they wanted to annoy him. There are probably certain dimensions to it that I know nothing about.

Next to the police headquarters was the *Kommandantur*, which housed the police of the Wehrmacht. We hostages, all students under the age of twenty-one, had to sign our names there every day. If we didn't, our parents would be made hostages in our place, so we couldn't leave Paris at all.

LA: Were some of the hostages killed, or did this threat stop the attacks on the Germans?

FG: In time, many hostages were executed or sent to concentration camps, but not right then. In addition to the hostages in line at the police headquarters, there were some Jews and English people. Since the English were at war with the Germans, if they were still on French territory, they had to line up and sign their names every day. At first, they were still free. Later, they were put into camps. I had an American friend who was free until the Americans entered the war, but after that she was put into a camp.

We French hostages figured out right away that since we were hostages because we were students, we could stop being hostages by no longer being students. My father went to the French police, and I guess he must have given them some money, too. He had papers drawn up to show that I was no longer a student, that I worked in fashion. My father wanted me to be able to escape if I had to. So they changed my status to that of an employee for a *maison de couture*. Haute couture was protected, at least temporarily. The Germans didn't want more French lawyers, but fashion seemed harmless to them.

After two or three months, almost all the French students found a way out of the hostage situation, either by pretending they were farmers or by finding some occupation that was acceptable to both the Abwehr and the Vichy government. We just disappeared into the woodwork.

In Neuilly, I don't know anyone who was killed from that first group, whereas in some of the suburbs hostages were killed later on because they belonged to the Resistance. They were jailed and then executed in a military fort called Mont-Valérien, where there is a very important memorial to all those who died during the Nazi occupation and also to those who fought and died with de Gaulle.

I did design models for Lucien Lelong. It was more a pretense than a reality, but the pretense served my purposes because for the first time I could use that studio at my grandmother's house to produce something. As a matter of fact, I started to paint seriously. It also allowed me to travel to the free zone. If I could go to the free zone, then I could escape if I had to. Nineteen forty was such a bad year, with the total defeat in the spring.

In 1941, I started making things for fashion that earned me some money, like buttons in ceramic, since there were no more buttons in Paris. Also earrings. I sold them to fashion houses and to a woman named Line Vautrin. At that time, she worked mostly in enamel on copper, not only jewelry items, but also powder containers—

minaudières. Also, beautiful mirrors. Her mother and she had a shop in Paris.

Also in 1941, I encountered the painter Endre Rozsda, whom I had first met in September 1939. He always got up at noon, so he said I could use his studio to paint from 9:00 a.m. to noon. I started working at his place while he slept. When he woke up, he often gave me some criticism. Then I worked at my own studio in the afternoon or sat for him, since he wanted to make my portrait.

So this was when I started painting seriously in oil. I had done my first oil painting in 1939. Until then, I had been doing mostly watercolors and drawings. As soon as I tried oil, I knew it was the medium for me. You can rework an oil painting much more easily than a watercolor. If you're not satisfied with a watercolor, you have to do another. Whereas you can work on an oil for months, even years! It corresponded more to my temperament. It could absorb more passion without getting destroyed.

LA: So you were now painting in the studio that had been your playroom and, before that, your mother's studio. What had become of the War Room turned sewing room?

FG: It was no longer the sewing room because my grandfather had died when I was eleven and the sewing machine had been moved to his bedroom on a lower floor.

LA: That's interesting, don't you think? The sewing room was moved to any room that represented death, in order to restore life to it.

FG: That's true. Maybe to mend life, to sew it together again. The War Room was on the third floor, and the sewing room was switched from there to the room in the exact

Self-portrait by Françoise, 1941, graphite, 20" x 19"
(now at the Metropolitan Museum in New York)

same location on the second floor. The ex–War Room became my bedroom, and it was still sinister, with the pictures of all the destruction still on the walls.

LA: That's incredible. The war ended in 1918, and you took it over as your bedroom in 1934, and those ghastly photos were still there?

FG: The War Room became my bedroom when I was twelve, and I slept there when I was visiting my maternal grandmother. But by then, I was used to it, so I didn't change it right away. I left my parents' house in 1943 and started living at my grandmother's. But I couldn't bear that bedroom anymore because another war was now going on.

I put all those photos and souvenirs of destruction in a large suitcase and repainted the walls in white, with a depiction of Dionysus above the mantel. Dionysus was arriving in a landscape beside the sea where Ariadne slept, supposedly almost dead after Theseus's desertion. She believes her life is over, and she's in such despair that she swoons. He resurrects her, and she becomes a constellation.

Dionysus was standing with a faun beside him, very linear. The painting was five feet high by four feet wide. At that time, I always identified with Ariadne and with the thread that allows people to get through the labyrinth of human destiny. Dionysus was a very important character to me too, because I thought the poetic impulse had to be not just Apollonian but Dionysian, involving madness as well as reason. Passion. Going to the extreme. Passion was my thing.

For my mural, I picked the moment when Dionysus arrives from the spiritual side, the left side. And to the right, lying down, is Ariadne asleep. I first painted it in

1942. Then I redid it, more simplified, in 1944. I even signed some of my paintings Ariane [the French spelling of the name] at that time.

LA: What was the tragedy in your life at that point that made you identify with her?

FG: I think it was the theme of death and resurrection that I responded to and also finding oneself amid that disastrous, catastrophic war. The theme was more fundamental than being based on any one person or relationship.

LA: Existential.

FG: Yes. Also, I identified with both Dionysus and Ariadne. And Dionysus-Ariadne is a more interesting archetype to me than Theseus-Ariadne. After all, Theseus is only a man. After he leaves her stranded, the one who comes to her is a god, and he turns her into a constellation.

So I think it was the metaphysical aspect of the myth that appealed most to me. Later, from 1961 to 1963, I explored the same theme in completely abstract composition in about fifty paintings. That myth seems to be fundamental for me. Theseus and the Minotaur, as well as Dionysus and Ariadne, are all part of myself.

Even as a child, I did small drawings of Dionysus. I was attracted to him because he embodied the aspect of inspiration that involved going completely berserk, as opposed to Apollonian inspiration, which involves harmony, self-knowledge, et cetera. It was the myth that appealed to me most. It's so complete.

When I took it on again in 1961, I went from the birth

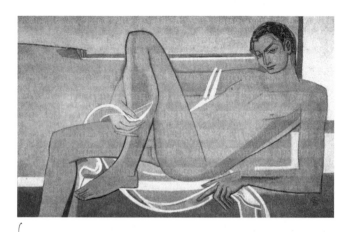

Dionysos, Françoise Gilot, 1987, oil on canvas,
32" x 51¼"

of Ariadne and Theseus onward, each important moment of their lives being a painting.

LA: It's an interesting myth in Freudian terms as well—the Minotaur as the id, Theseus as the superego, Ariadne as the self, and . . .

FG: Dionysus as the godhead. It covers every level of the psyche. That's why it's the fundamental archetype for my type of psyche. The mural in the War Room is the first time I painted it. In that sense, it was, again, like an exorcism.

It's really silly that I didn't photograph it because it was one of my best works. It was in just white and ochers. Later, when I painted Dionysus in 1987, it was again with very little color. In my most important paintings, there is little color.

LA: Yet you're considered a colorist.

FG: But when I get to my archetypes, I don't use color.

LA: You've said that your impulse now is to do white paintings?

FG: I'm already not in the mood I was in when I said that. I was so discouraged then that I didn't paint. And when you don't paint, the paintings that should have been done during that period don't surge. It's very strange.

LA: I've noticed that with writing, too. If you don't do it when it grabs you by the throat, it doesn't get done. You have to strike while the iron is hot.

FG: Yes, because you have to feel the passion linked to it. That's where Dionysus comes in.

So if I exorcised the terror of World War I through transforming the War Room into my studio, how did you deal with the terror of World War II that you must have absorbed as an infant?

LA: Through home theater, I think. When I was growing up, I had three brothers. On the street behind us were three more boys and two girls. That was our core group, and there were several others who came and went. In the summer, we played together all day every day. Mainly what we did was act out stories about, as I realize looking back, various aspects of American history.

One scenario involved a pioneer family. We had a mother, a father, and several young children. I was usually a brother. Some neighbors had a small playhouse in their backyard, with windows, a door, a peaked roof. That was our pioneer cabin. We assembled various outfits—fringed leather jackets, coonskin caps, moccasins.

All day long, we devised adventures that would happen to this family. We had toy rifles and went buffalo hunting. We perched on the peaked roof as floodwaters rose around us. We boarded up the windows and door as tornadoes approached or Indians attacked. People lost limbs. Babies died. It was very catastrophic, a childhood soap opera.

Of course the actual tragedy was that those who settled America slaughtered those who were already here, both the animals and the Native Americans, and seized their lands. We knew that our ancestry included both the settlers and the natives, the oppressors and the victims. Our father always told us that he, and therefore we, had

Lisa wandering the woods at the age of four.

Cherokee ancestors. So we were probably trying to figure out where our sympathies lay—with the cowboys or with the Indians.

Another game we played, usually in my backyard, involved a Cherokee tribe. The older boys could join an Indian club that a father down the street ran. They ordered rawhide, feathers, beads, and so on by mail and made ankle bracelets, armbands, headdresses, loincloths. Twenty or more boys—with the older men directing things. Sort of an early *Iron John* experience. They built a large tepee in the woods and held ceremonial dances around campfires.

No girls were allowed, so we used to steal our brothers' supplies to make our own costumes. Then the girls and the younger boys danced around campfires in my backyard. We had a tribe with a chief, squaws, and warriors. I was usually a warrior or sometimes the chief. I always got to do the best dances because it was my backyard! The Dying Eagle dance was my specialty, for which I'd made feathered wings, a loincloth, a headdress. I swooped and flailed and fluttered around the campfire and ended up dead on the ground. It might have been my homage to my Cherokee ancestors.

We also played Civil War, turning the toolshed off our garage into a hospital. We had gray Confederate caps and blue Yankee ones, with little crossed sabers on the bills. We had guns and blue or gray outfits we'd assembled from bits and pieces. Nobody wanted to be a Yankee because we thought of ourselves as southerners, so we forced the little children to be Yankees if they wanted to play with us. We conducted big battles and slaughtered each other.

Then we adjourned to our hospital, where we took off our blue and gray, put on white, and became doctors and nurses and patients. We put red food coloring in bottles of water for blood, and then we ran strings from the bottles and taped them to the patients' arms for transfusions.

My father gave us free samples from drug companies, making sure that we cleaned the medicine out of the capsules. Then we concocted remedies out of sugar and flour to refill the capsules, which we made the patients swallow. We did mock operations with dinner knives and forks. We had masks and caps my father had given us from the operating room. It was a very serious business, but you wouldn't have wanted to be a patient in our hospital, I assure you.

FG: The younger ones were the patients?

LA: Of course. It was the only way we let them play with us. Often when people talk about "playing doctor" as children, they mean exploring each other sexually. But we really meant it! We splinted limbs and bandaged wounds with all this tape and gauze my father gave us. We had crutches for those who had lost legs. I suppose you could regard it as childhood S/M!

FG: He probably gave you all those supplies in the hope that you'd become physicians yourselves.

LA: Yes, and it worked. Two of my brothers and my sister are now doctors. Unfortunately, I had a serious blood disease when I was seven and developed a blood phobia, so I couldn't participate in this family métier.

We also played World War II. At that time, the cereal companies, as a bribe to get children to force their parents to buy those brands, put a packet inside each box containing replicas of World War II uniform patches. We had a huge variety of them.

At the army-navy store, you could buy olive drab or camouflage jackets, onto which we sewed our patches. My father's old uniforms were in the attic. He was a captain, so we used his hats, which hung down over our eyes. We crawled all around the neighborhood on our bellies cradling toy rifles.

Later, during the Korean War, the father of a boy on a street behind ours was killed, and we were all very upset for him. The newspapers were full of stories about American prisoners of war and the tortures and brainwashing to which they were being subjected. We kids discussed how to avoid breaking under torture. I used to practice staying underwater in the deep end of the swimming pool for that purpose. I worked up to one minute before the lifeguards made me stop.

During this time, we were conducting skirmishes with some older kids in our neighborhood. At one point, they captured me and tied me to a grape arbor. As they discussed how to torture me, I was giving myself pep talks about how I was not going to betray my comrades, no matter what they did to me. Luckily, my courageous resolve was never tested, because our mothers called us home to lunch.

Whenever my mother wanted us to come home, she'd stand outside the back door and whistle a certain refrain, and we'd come running from all over the neighborhood. I was never so happy to hear her whistle as I was that day.

All these dramas must have been a way for us to deal with what we were discussing in history class at school and hearing about around our dinner tables at night. Maybe it fulfilled the same function as sewing and painting in the War Room did for you. It was a way to tame the violence, to bring it down to a personal level at which we could begin to comprehend it and cope with it.

FG: Children want to experiment with what they regard as the real world. Also, adults don't realize how much they speak about things like war. Children have to find out what it's like, if only in a make-believe way.

LA: World War II had dominated the early lives of most of my playmates. Their fathers had been away fighting in Europe or the Pacific. In our attic, we had stacks of *Life* magazines my mother had saved that had pictures of all the destruction in Europe, and we used to look through them, completely bewildered. I think crawling around the neighborhood on our bellies with rifles cradled in our arms was our way of trying to make sense of something so senseless.

Throughout my childhood, America and Russia, Britain and France, were exploding atomic and hydrogen bombs hither and yon. At school, we were taught how to hide beneath our flimsy little desks in case the Communists bombed our classroom.

When I was in high school, my parents turned part of our basement into a fallout shelter. At dinner, we used to discuss whether or not we'd let our less prepared neighbors come into our shelter once the bomb fell, like lazy grasshoppers seeking refuge with us industrious ants.

My father used to muse that the atomic bombs that had slaughtered and maimed and poisoned so many Japanese had perhaps saved his life, since he was on a troopship bound for the South Pacific—where many men he knew had already been killed—when Japan surrendered. Whether propaganda or not, Japanese soldiers, rather than respecting the red crosses on medical personnel, were rumored to have used them as targets instead. He pointed out that my brothers Bill and Michael might not even exist without those ghastly bombs.

A phantom bomb was ever present in my childhood, hovering overhead like the vengeful God of the Old Testament. My twenties were dominated by the Vietnam War. It was the height of the back-to-the-land movement in Vermont, and there were some two hundred communes. Many people, including my ex-husband and me, had moved there thinking we needed to know how to provide for our own needs in order to have at least a chance of surviving when the bombs fell or when the cities became uninhabitable from all the environmental toxins and catastrophes. Many in the communes were working on antiwar projects. I took my daughter, Sara, in her stroller to marches in Burlington.

Then came Desert Storm, the war in Iraq, the Afghan War. It's a nightmare that seems never ending.

2. THE VIRGINIA CLUB

LA: If your childhood was aesthetic, mine was ascetic, not because we didn't have money, but because my parents were abstemious. My mother was supposedly descended from Puritans who arrived in America on the *Mayflower*, fleeing religious persecution in England.

Or rather, this is the branch of her family she most identified with. Those ancestors were ministers, farmers, lawyers, suffragists, and they felt it was sinful to be concerned with material objects, including clothing. My mother, for example, had one good dress when I was a child, of rose and ivory brocade, which she wore to every cocktail party and dinner party for years.

If I needed a dress for a dance, the way I was taught to shop was to go to the three clothing stores in town—it was a small town of fewer than twenty thousand people at that time—and see what was available in my size, and then buy the cheapest, preferably on sale. My preferences or what looked good on me didn't enter into the equation.

But that was my mother. My father was a Virginian. His family was Southern Baptist, which in theory is a rigid faith that proscribes drinking, dancing, card playing, erotic pleasure outside marriage. But in reality Southern Baptists are very passionate people, as I know firsthand from having been on hayrides the Baptist youth group used to sponsor!

My Southern Baptist grandmother, my father's mother, was very concerned with her appearance, despite warnings from the preachers about the hellfire that awaited those who succumbed to worldly vanities. She was always beautifully dressed and accessorized. But my mother regarded her as a bit superficial. I identified with my mother, so I never paid much attention to clothes, apart from trying to fit in with my classmates and not stand out in any way.

Mine was a sensuous upbringing in that we had an intense relationship to nature—flowers, animals, insects, fish, the forests and skies and fields of the southern Appalachians. My father owned farms in remote spots, on which he raised tobacco, corn, dairy cattle, and beef cattle. Fascinating things to do with the natural world were going on all the time. Fashion was at the bottom of my list.

FG: Whether the attitude is for or against, personal grooming is a product of one's culture.

LA: This antipathy toward it wasn't the general attitude. Most southern women place great emphasis upon being well turned out. But because I adored my mother, who was from upstate New York, I tried to honor her very different value system.

FG: When you were growing up, did you do anything for yourself like knit?

LA: I sewed a full skirt one time from polished cotton with a pattern of Chinese pagodas, which were supposed to rim the skirt. When I finished, my pagodas arced up the skirt like the path of the rising sun and then plunged off the bottom. After that, I gave up. My goal was not to make an individual statement but rather to look exactly like everyone else.

FG: At school in France, we also wanted to look like everybody else. We wore kilts and boys' style shirts or jerseys, mostly from a store called Old England. But the party dresses for special occasions were supposed to be individual statements. On Sunday, we went for lunch to my paternal grandmother's with all my cousins, aunts, and uncles, and for that you had to be well dressed. During afternoons off from school, we would see other children, and for those occasions we had to dress up. But at school, we even wore black pinafores.

LA: Did the really popular girls wear their school hats or ties in some distinctive way that everyone else copied?

FG: One year, I came back from England with a marvelous blue feather, maybe nine inches long. I decided it would look wonderful along the side of my felt uniform hat, as in Austria. Two hundred of us were standing in a large hall waiting for the headmistress to arrive, and I was the only one with a feather in my cap.

Right away, she pointed at me and called, "What is this feather doing on your hat?"

I had to give it to her. My classmates had been saying, "How long is it going to be tolerated?" No one imagined it would last such a short time.

LA: So my mother felt clothes were for covering the body—fashion minimalism, so to speak. It bothered my father,

Lisa's mother, Alice Greene (Reed), modeling "a little black dress" (1937).

whose mother was a clotheshorse. My mother, when they were courting, had been a model for Eastman Kodak. I have photos of her in lovely gowns. A Hollywood scout passing through her town had singled her out as a future movie star. This forecast was written up in the local newspaper along with her photo. I don't know what happened after she got to Tennessee to make her lose interest in all that.

FG: Before her marriage, your mother was earning money by showing clothes and being photographed. Then she got married and lost interest, but not because of her husband, who might have been drawn to her partly because she was so elegant.

LA: He often talked with pride about the various men over whom he'd won out. He loved that she was beautiful. Not long before he died, at age ninety-five, he referred to her as a "classic beauty."

FG: I've seen her photographs. She was very pretty, so psychologically it would be interesting to know what happened to her between being a young woman and then being married and having children.

LA: I think motherhood wasn't her preferred vocation. She did fine in terms of providing food and clothing and a nice place to live. But her heart wasn't really in it. She always told us that the most important thing in life was to do your duty. But if she had any time left over from her duties, she wanted to be left alone to read. She said late in life that she wished she'd been a history professor.

Once I became a mother myself, I understood. Caring for just one child was challenging enough for me. I couldn't imagine having five. So I think she went into a depression and didn't emerge until we all left home.

She also said she thought living in the South would be moonlight and magnolias. Instead, she found herself in a factory town full of people she didn't really understand. Letting her appearance go might have been her form of protest.

FG: Puritanism might have been just an excuse. That's why one's attitude toward clothes is not neutral.

LA: My grandmother and my mother disliked each other. By repudiating clothes, maybe my mother was repudiating her mother-in-law.

FG: Do you see the articulation between womanhood and being pro or con fashion? It's not a superficial reason that made your mother decide that fashion was superficial!

LA: It might also have been retaliation against my father for his being so fixated on her appearance. Maybe she wanted to be loved for her true self, not just her surface presentation. But in reality, he adored everything about her.

Sometimes I also felt she was sending me a message: "Don't let this happen to you." From being a celebrated beauty, courted and catered to, she became the mother of five, dealing with laundry and groceries, economically dependent on a husband she rarely saw. I heard the message loud and clear. I have one child and a career. Not that being a celebrated beauty was ever one of my options!

FG: The fact of your mother's saying no to fashion gives such a contrast to my own experience. My family said yes.

LA: My father was so upset by her self-neglect that at one point he gave me money to buy her clothes. So I bought her a hat, a coat, a couple of outfits. She took them all back for a refund.

For her seventieth birthday, I got my siblings to contribute toward a beautiful camel hair coat for her, since she didn't even own an overcoat. But she returned that for a refund, too.

I used to send her my clothes when I got tired of them. So she wore my old clothes, and those of a friend of mine, and sometimes those of her sisters.

FG: That's strange, because your mother was about half your size. After a certain age, my mother did that with me. Even though she had the most beautiful clothes herself, many times she wanted to wear my old clothes. It was bizarre because I am at least one size smaller, so she had to have them enlarged by a seamstress. I never understood why my mother would want my things, especially since she was much more affluent than I.

My daughter Paloma could buy any cashmere sweater she wanted, but as a teenager she preferred to borrow mine. Later I began to wear clothes she no longer wanted. We are the same size, so that's less hard to understand. Whereas with your mother and you, it was absurd! And with my mother and me, it was absurd in the other direction.

LA: My mother would say that they're perfectly good clothes that aren't worn-out yet. That would be her conscious motive, but her unconscious one, and maybe your mother's too, would be . . .

FG: To assimilate themselves to us.

LA: Your mother painted but not professionally. And my mother wrote wonderful letters but didn't write as a career. Her brief career was teaching literature, and all her life she read books avidly. I probably wanted to write partly to try to please and interest her.

FG: Even our Paleolithic ancestors wore furs, scrubbed the leather to make it smoother, and ornamented it with beads, so fashion didn't begin yesterday. These things we call ornamental or decorative are actually fundamental to humankind. The stances people take with regard to fashion aren't superficial. Important things are going on psychologically.

LA: My paternal grandmother was from Virginia, and she and some friends from Virginia formed the Virginia Club. They met monthly to discuss how lucky they were not to be Tennesseans. They dressed beautifully and served elaborate food on lovely china. Sometimes they talked nostalgically about the way things used to be before the War Between the States.

FG: And they certainly were not even born then.

LA: No, they would have been born a couple of decades after the Civil War. They would have heard about it from their parents and grandparents. I guess it was partly an attempt to preserve the positive aspects of that culture that had been destroyed. In a sense, they were trying to transcend the devastation of war, the same as with your War Room.

FG: So many lives have been lost in wars. What is of interest is the way in which women's memories reenact those disasters, to assimilate them into culture, to tame the grief and the horror, and to ensure the survival of historical facts and their meaning, so that the lessons are not altogether lost. Your grandmother continued the retelling of stories from her parents and grandparents as a tradition that had to be passed on.

LA: But my grandmother's reality was that she was from southwest Virginia, a coal-mining region, and she grew up on a little farm in the hills, not on a plantation. Some of her ancestors had come from Tidewater Virginia, but they had probably been indentured servants, not plantation owners. She was a mountain girl, not a southern belle. Yet she went to these meetings and presented herself as one.

Even in her nursing home in her nineties, she wore skirts to her knees, high heels, and full-battle makeup. It's a good example of the axiom that you can become who you say you are. She came from the coalfields and became a Tidewater lady. It's the female version of the American Dream, rags to riches. Rags to Ricci. She may be the one who gave me my taste for fiction, because her whole life was a fiction.

By the end, I think my grandmother believed that she was who she claimed to be. It's taken me a long time to realize that she wasn't. And it's taken me even longer to realize that maybe she *was*! Because who's to say what's reality? The scientific discoveries of the twentieth century suggest that there is no such thing as objective external "reality."

FG: For women, acquiring status has always had a lot to do with ornamenting their bodies. If your ambition was to rise in society, dressing the part was one way to become who you wanted to be.

LA: Think about Lily Bart in Edith Wharton's *House of Mirth*—how an observer could gauge her mental, economic, and moral decline by the decline in her toilette.

FG: She's less wealthy than the people around her, but she's more elegant, and that's why they invite her. Except that novel is set at the turn of the twentieth century, whereas in France it was still that way not so long ago.

In Wharton's *Glimpses of the Moon*, the young couple get married and think they are going to continue to be professional guests, but eventually they become so poor that they can't maintain the fiction. She is redeemed when she refuses to marry a wealthy man she doesn't love and goes to live with a family in a modest area to help out with their children. For the first time, she's true to herself and her real feelings, and she finds love again.

In French society—you can see it in Balzac's novels—it's through their clothes that many people move from one layer of society to another. So appearance can function as a vehicle.

I was entirely conscious, even when I was quite young, that with a bit of care, my appearance could be impeccable. Children can be very cruel, and when you go to a party at which you know no one, what you are wearing is your only protection.

LA: That's true. It's your armor, like a shell for a lobster.

FG: Each time I was going somewhere as a child, I made sure that my nails were white, white, white, so that the parents of the children I was visiting wouldn't think that I was untidy.

LA: So that's two ways of using clothing in my family: my

mother as a way to protest her situation, and my grandmother as a way to reinvent herself.

FG: We've talked about how women, mostly through story-
telling, will have a decisive impact on the younger generations. It's their way of attempting to pass on history,
traditions, customs, manners. Sometimes they succeed,
and other times children revolt. I'd like to know more in
this regard about your Virginia grandmother.

LA: When my grandmother got to Tennessee, she built
a large Georgian house in brick with columns out front.
After my father came back from the war, we returned to
Tennessee, and my grandparents gave us their house. They
bought another one, high on a hill outside town, overlook-
ing a river. Across the river was the country club and golf
course. It had been a bootleggers' nightclub. There was a
veranda along the river with wonderful views of the mountains beyond the river.

FG: Matisse's mother advised people about their homes.
She became an interior decorator before the word existed,
and it gave him his taste for color. Your grandmother
became affluent, didn't she, since her husband was a physi-
cian?

LA: Yes. Both my grandfather's parents were dead by the
time he was ten. They left a thousand-acre farm, but his
uncle, the executor, sold it and squandered the proceeds,
leaving my grandfather an orphan without means. His
oldest sister took him in. Later, my grandfather ran away
to live with his two older brothers in Kentucky, who sent
him to a boarding high school there.

House built by Lisa's paternal grandparents in
Kingsport, Tennessee, in which Lisa grew up (1926).

My grandfather put himself through teachers college. He was my grandmother's teacher, as well as her second cousin. He had always dreamed of becoming a doctor. After they married, she said, "Do it."

So he went on scholarship to a premed program in Louisville, Kentucky, while she stayed in Virginia and taught school to support them. He hopped freight trains to visit her. Then he went to the Medical College of Virginia in Richmond, where he worked at the Robert E. Lee Camp Confederate Soldiers' Home, sold aluminum pots door-to-door, worked for a lumber company, and pitched for a semiprofessional baseball team.

She sold cosmetics in a department store. Then she became a teacher in a reform school for delinquent girls on the outskirts of Richmond. One day, she was walking to her carriage, and some girls who were unhappy with her surrounded her and began to attack her. She pulled a long hat pin from her hair and fought them off with it like a fencing foil until she could climb in her buggy and escape. But for hat pins, I wouldn't exist!

FG: I've seen hat pins belonging to my grandmother, and they could be twelve inches long. They really could serve as weapons.

LA: After my grandfather got his medical license, they went back to southwest Virginia, where my grandfather kept a stable of six horses for house calls into the mountains.

Then my grandparents heard about a new town being founded on the Holston River in Tennessee—Kingsport. This was in 1917. The South had been destroyed economically by the Civil War and its aftermath. Northern capitalists wanted to move their factories south from New

England to profit from the cheap, nonunionized labor, just as they're doing today vis-à-vis Asia.

FG: Is it what you describe in *Original Sins*?

LA: Yes. Kingsport was founded as a factory town for northern industry. There was a textile mill, a paper mill, a glass plant, a press, a chemical company, a munitions plant. Farmers came down out of the hills to work. My grandfather established the town's first two hospitals.

The Yankee plant managers were like the British in India. They built their houses on a ridge, with cottages down in the valley for the workers. My grandparents built up on the ridge.

Of course, it was déclassé to be Appalachian. So my grandmother played up her Virginia origins. It's more prestigious to be a Virginian than a Tennessean because Virginia has that Tidewater area around Jamestown, where the first English settlement in America occurred. Supposedly, the people who settled there were broken-down Cavaliers who'd been given land grants by James I.

FG: Why do you use that word "Tidewater"?

LA: Tidewater Virginia is the area along the Atlantic coastline that's fed by tidal rivers like the James, the York, the Rappahannock. Tidewater Virginia is an Anglican plantation culture, whereas southwest Virginia, my grandparents' homeland, is southern Appalachian mountain culture—Celtic, Scots-Irish, Border Reiver, Native American. So my grandmother led everyone to believe that her ancestors had received land grants from James I and that she was a Tidewater lady, not a mountain girl from a hardscrabble farm.

She and her friends went to club meetings every day of the week—a fancy luncheon followed by an educational program. In addition to the Virginia Club, she belonged to a garden club, a Bible-study club, a book club, a music club, several bridge clubs, Junior League, and Delphians, which was a service club.

FG: All within the same house?

LA: No, it was different clubs with different members, but my grandmother belonged to them all—just to make sure that nothing was going on that she didn't know about. The meetings rotated among the houses of the different members.

Every day of the week, she dressed up, and her wardrobe was fantastic. She could arrange flowers, she cooked well, she was a gracious hostess. She bought antiques, Oriental carpets, beautiful fabrics, and at night she upholstered her furniture and sewed her curtains. She was a force of nature!

FG: Can you describe her color scheme?

LA: At her second house, the bootleggers' nightclub, there were windows all along one wall of the living room with views of the river and mountains. Her color scheme there was rose and turquoise. She had a huge Aubusson carpet in those tones that ran the length of the room. The sofas were rose; the Queen Anne wing chairs were covered in satin striped with gold, turquoise, and rose.

Her dining room wallpaper featured the docks in Charleston with happy slaves loading bales of cotton onto a sailing ship. But my grandmother wouldn't have known a cotton boll if one had landed in her soup.

FG: When you were a child, was she already a widow?

LA: No, my grandfather was alive, but he often avoided her because she was always trying to mold him into a southern gentleman. He was an innately sweet, polite, and courtly man—tall and slender with very blue eyes. When my father was shipped off to Europe during World War II, my grandfather gave me a lot of attention, and we were very close during my childhood.

My grandmother made sure his shirts were silk, with his monogram on the pockets. They traveled a lot, always first-class. But my grandfather's real love was golf. He'd tee up in the side yard of their house and drive his ball across the river to the golf course. Then he'd go down the hill to the river, where he kept a little boat. He'd row across the river, locate his ball, and play on around the course. And my grandmother wouldn't even know he was gone.

He was also a ladies' man. Rumor had it that my grandmother ran several attractive nurses out of town.

FG: Your father grew up in the first house, the one with the columns?

LA: Yes, they moved there when he was eleven. He went to the local schools. But everybody living on the ridge thought of the North as the mother country. So it was impressed upon him that he should go north to college and then come home to serve his people.

Eastman Kodak has a chemical factory in Kingsport, so there were strong ties between Kingsport and Rochester, New York, where the headquarters is located. George Eastman, the founder of the corporation, arranged scholarships at the University of Rochester for local boys he considered promising, including my father. So my father met my mother there. The daughter of a lawyer, she had grown up in Rochester and was attending that university, as did her four sisters.

Then my father went to Harvard Medical School, while my mother taught high school English in upstate New York. After they married, he did his residency at the Roosevelt Hospital in New York. My older brother was born at the French Hospital in New York, and I was conceived on West Fifty-Eighth Street, ten blocks from my current apartment. Like a salmon, I've returned to my spawning grounds.

FG: So you're a New Yorker after all?

LA: Yes, my grandmother would have been so appalled to realize this!

FG: You described how your grandmother became who she imagined herself to be. Now let's examine how she handed on who she was, or had become, to the next generation. She impressed upon your father the desirability of going north to school to become a doctor. What about the next generation—her grandchildren?

LA: We had dinner there every Sunday after church. She and my grandfather were Southern Baptists, and she was very staunch. My grandfather had a beautiful singing voice and sang in a gospel quartet.

My father, having been raised Southern Baptist, was terrified as a child by all the sermons about burning forever in lakes of molten flame, so he was determined not to subject his children to that. My mother had been a Congregationalist in Rochester. The early Puritans of New

England had morphed into Congregationalists. But there was no Congregational church in Kingsport, so we went to the Episcopal one.

My grandmother used to take me aside and say, "Your father has been very sad and lost ever since he fell away from the Baptist faith."

Anyway, we'd go to the Episcopal church, and my grandparents would go to the Baptist one, and afterward we'd have a conciliatory lunch at their house. Or we might go out to our farm instead, where we had a log cabin from pioneer days, and then at night we'd have dinner with my grandparents.

FG: You were how many people at the table?

LA: My grandparents, parents, and four kids. My younger sister wasn't born until I was fourteen. Those meals were sometimes tense, since my mother and my grandmother didn't get along. My grandmother encouraged my father to go north for college because that was prestigious among her friends, but she had planned on his marrying her best friend's daughter, whom he had dated in high school. When he didn't, she at least expected my mother to strive to be more like herself—to go to club meetings and to lavish attention on her appearance.

FG: Maybe your mother thought the social set there was less fashionable than what she'd come from. For instance, if I'm in New York or Paris, I dress up automatically. But if I go to Brittany, I don't feel obliged to do the same.

LA: It wasn't so much that those Kingsport women weren't fashionable. They didn't work outside their homes, and they often had hired help, so they put all their energy

Lisa, at age eleven, with her parents and brothers.

into being beautiful and charming. That was their way of expressing themselves.

FG: Do you have any idea why your mother refused to join this fashion parade?

LA: I think she always had a sense of superiority, not in terms of her appearance, but in terms of her intelligence. She was a very bright woman—number one in her class at the university. Other women in Kingsport were plenty smart, but they did their best to conceal it because that's the southern way—to act dumb even when you're not. And they were so intent on being charming that they rarely said what they really thought. So there was always a certain tension in their presence as you tried to decipher their true meanings. My mother often preferred to stay home and read a book instead.

One time, my parents and I were discussing diets, and I asked how much water weighed. Without a moment's hesitation, she replied, "Eight and a third pounds to the gallon." My father and I just looked at her with amazement. I never asked her a question of fact that she couldn't answer. She read the *Encyclopaedia Britannica* twice for her own entertainment! She had an analytical mind and a great love of learning and of abstract discussion. She also had a keen sense of irony. As an outsider in that town, she had a wry take on everything that happened there.

FG: Which you have used quite well in the satirical parts of your novels.

LA: That's from her. My father also had a good sense of humor, but his was much more earthy and slapstick, a southern sense of humor. He was also gifted at telling stories.

FG: You said there was a certain amount of puritanism in your mother, which perhaps became more evident once she was a wife and mother. Was there something about her roots that might explain this?

LA: That's an interesting idea—that she might have reverted to family norms once she had a family of her own. Her mother's family was Scots-Irish and Anglo-Irish. The Scots are well-known for being parsimonious. The Anglo-Irish branch might have been abstemious by necessity, because they came to America around the time of the potato famine.

Two branches of her father's mother's family were Huguenots who fled France after the revocation of the Edict of Nantes.

There were also some Puritans who supposedly came to Massachusetts on the *Mayflower*. Many Americans claim their families came over on the *Mayflower*, but I think mine really did. My great-grandmother, my mother's father's mother, was a staff genealogist for the Daughters of the American Revolution, and she did a family tree that includes every leaf. In addition to the DAR, she had enough credentials to belong to the Daughters of Founders and Patriots of America, the Daughters of the Cincinnati, the Mayflower Society, the Order of the Crown, the Colonial Daughters of the Seventeenth Century, and the Colonial Dames.

So my mother got puritanical blood from several directions—the Huguenots, the Puritans, the Scots, and the Anglo-Irish.

FG: So in her eyes less was always better?

LA: Her favorite saying was "Use it up, wear it out, make it do, or do without." And my father didn't help much. He didn't like to spend money. They had four small children and a fifth later on, and I think he was in a financial panic with all that new responsibility. But the combination of present circumstances and my mother's family background was deadly for her.

FG: What was your Virginia grandmother's relationship to you?

LA: My contact with her was mostly via our Sunday lunches. She lived outside town, and until I could drive, I couldn't go see her on my own. But she was often in town for club meetings and would stop by in her big silver Cadillac. One time, I came home from school and found her going through my parents' mail. She never wanted anything going on that she didn't know about!

What she tried to impress upon us was, first of all, the importance of being Southern Baptist. And second, the importance of being southern ladies and gentlemen. One of her clubs sponsored the Symphony Ball each year. When the daughters and granddaughters of the members reached sixteen, they took waltz classes. We wore white Scarlett O'Hara gowns with hoopskirts and kid gloves reaching above our elbows.

FG: And this was the 1960s? The historical nostalgia expressed in the costumes is stunning.

LA: At the time, it was just what we did. It never occurred to us how bizarre it was.

FG: Nineteen sixty? Eight years before 1968. That was the time of the Beat Generation, but where you were, it was still debutante balls. Think of that!

LA: What's even more interesting is what it says about how people fictionalize their lives. That region of Tennessee is part of Appalachia, and many men there fought with the Union army during the Civil War. It's very mountainous, and there weren't big plantations; hence, there weren't a lot of slaves. Even now, the black population of our town is only about 7 percent. When Tennessee seceded from the United States, east Tennessee tried, unsuccessfully, to secede from Tennessee so as to remain with the Union.

My grandmother's grandfather was a sergeant in the Union army. Several of my grandfather's forebears, belonging to the Church of the Brethren and being abolitionists and pacifists, moved from Virginia to Kentucky to avoid fighting for the Confederacy. But my grandmother identified with the Confederacy.

In addition, genetic tests on my father indicate that my grandparents might have had a few Melungeon ancestors. The Melungeons, some claim, were living in our region when European settlers arrived. They had dark skin, and they were persecuted for the next two centuries, pushed off their land, not allowed to vote or to marry whites or to attend white schools or to testify against whites in court. They were thought to be the result of mixing among natives, mountain whites, escaped slaves, and free blacks. They themselves claimed to be Portuguese Indians (as did a grandmother of each of my grandparents). But nobody could figure out why Portuguese would be living in those mountains, so they were accused of using the claim of Portuguese ancestry to try to conceal their African origins.

Genetic research on their descendants suggests that

they were, in fact, of Mediterranean descent, as well as of Native American, African, northern European, Middle Eastern, and South Asian origins. After slavery became established in North America, anyone with darker skin was subject to being seized and sold as a slave. So many headed for the mountains and hid out with those under similar threat.

FG: How did you learn about the Melungeons?

LA: My father was reading a book by an author who maintained that he was a Melungeon descendant. He described the different branches of his family tree, and one branch turned out to be on my father's family tree, too. On both sides, since my father's father and mother, being second cousins, shared those same ancestors. There are several theories about Melungeon origins that I examined in my memoir *Kinfolks*. It's a complicated story.

But whatever their origins, a couple of hundred thousand people in our region and beyond are thought to be of Melungeon descent. Certain surnames recur in the records—Gibson, Mullins, Bowling, Collins, Goins, Bunch, several others.

My grandmother might have tried to escape the stigma of being Melungeon by moving out of the mountains, into a new town where no one knew anything about her except what she chose to tell them. This could explain why she never took us back to where she'd grown up and rarely introduced us to our relatives, even those who lived in our same town.

My father thought his parents distanced themselves from their homeland in southwest Virginia because it was so violent and alcoholic. My grandfather had almost been shot before they left, for aiding a cousin during a fight with a local bully, and many people there drank moonshine as though it were water.

Before I ever heard of Melungeons, I thought maybe my grandparents left there because they were ashamed of being Cherokee. One of my grandmother's aunts used to discuss being Cherokee with my father when he was a boy. But when I was a child, she'd learned it was unfashionable and denied it.

So my grandmother had a lot of different ancestries from which to choose—English, Dutch, German, Cherokee, Melungeon, with whatever ethnicities that may involve. She decided to go with the English strand and transfer it from the mountains to the Tidewater. She used to call the Virginia Club members "those fine Colonial ladies." She was living a fiction. I guess we all are. But let's call it a dream, as the Hindus do.

FG: So there's the genetic DNA and the "cultural DNA." Nature and nurture. She selected what she wanted to hand down to you and your brothers. As you say, it's partly fictional, but it's also precisely how evolution works. At birth, in each individual, even though thousands of genes are present, some are activated and some lie dormant. With nurture, meaning culture, certain traits are encouraged and others repressed. Nature operates a certain amount of selection, activating some genes and not others, and culture accentuates the process.

LA: Yes, there's an array of possibilities, yet it's an idea in someone's head that determines what the reality will become. My grandfather from the backwoods wanted to be a doctor. Maybe it came from watching helplessly as his parents died. It was an unlikely dream for an orphan without means. But somehow he made it happen, and it determined the rest of his life—and my father's life and my own life. My grandmother had it in *her* head to be a grand Virginia lady, so she brought that into being.

FG: Life becomes theatrical. We superimpose our choices on the given patterns. We become the comedians of our own destiny, or the tragedians, depending on our inclinations.

LA: With the appropriate costumes. Think about my glamorous grandmother and her stage set—her beautiful house filled with antiques, china, and silver.

FG: Those were the attributes necessary to create that reality. When you went to see her, did she impress upon you the need to dress the part? And when you appeared in an old T-shirt, did she dislike it?

LA: Right.

FG: Was your grandmother worried that your mother wouldn't teach you these things? Even though she could have, since she had been a model.

LA: Maybe. I do think my grandmother tried to soften my parents' abstemiousness. But it annoyed my mother and father, who felt she was spoiling us. She traveled a lot and brought back elaborate gifts, often something folkloric from whatever country she'd visited. And she always gave us large checks for Christmas and birthdays.

FG: What did you feel yourself?

LA: I felt conflicted because I was happy to have the money, but I knew my parents were angry. We turned the checks over to my father, and he probably put them into our college accounts. Or he might have put them back into my grandmother's account. He thought she was too extravagant for her means. She might have been, too. I don't know what her means were. She certainly lived large by my parents' standards.

But at Christmas, my mother used to take us four children down to Woolworth's and give us each a dollar with which to buy all our presents. For instance, I might buy my father a can of shoe polish for ten cents. I know this sounds like something out of Dickens, but they felt that since it was the thought that counted, you might just as well think good thoughts while buying inexpensive gifts.

Once, I got my brothers to contribute from their savings to buy my mother a book from the best-seller list, since she loved books so much. But she returned it for a refund, saying that she preferred to check it out of the library for free.

It was a confusing childhood because we lived in a big house on the best street in town. Yet all these penny-pinching economies made us believe we were poised on the threshold of the county poorhouse. And then my grandmother would sail in in her Cadillac, dripping with jewelry and furs, bearing exotic gifts from Egypt.

But my parents' behavior was partly because we were surrounded by so much real poverty. When we drove out to our farms, we passed shacks sided with tar paper and roofed with metal soft drink signs. Gaunt adults and filthy toddlers stared at us from collapsing porches. The yards would be cluttered with junked cars, old tires, cast-off washing machines, piles of empty bottles and tin cans.

The women sometimes sewed their own dresses from cloth flour sacks, so the flour company made its sacks from a patterned material.

My father dealt with this hardship all day long in his medical practice. I worked at his office several summers. He charged three dollars per visit, and some people couldn't afford it, so they brought sacks of green beans, country hams, or homemade cakes in payment. My parents felt that in the face of all this suffering it was obscene to flaunt your good fortune. I agreed with them. I still do. But as an adult, I've been searching for some happy medium between this Albert Schweitzer mode and that of my Auntie Mame grandmother.

FG: What about your maternal grandmother?

LA: She lived in Rochester. We went up there every summer when I was a child. By the time I was old enough to be aware of her, she was either somewhat deaf or had atherosclerosis. She mostly just sat there smiling by the lake.

But in her day, she rode a bicycle before women did that. She worked as a secretary at an incubator company before she married. After she married, she had five daughters, and it sounds as though she went into a permanent depression. The only thing she enjoyed was organizing the sales and dinners at her church. She hated cooking and housework. Her spinster sister, a nurse who lived with them, did most of it, along with her daughters, my aunts. So that grandmother was fairly revolutionary in her youth, but marriage and motherhood damped her down—just as they seemed to my own mother.

FG: So the one who was foremost for you was your paternal grandmother, who could count for two.

My previous daughter-in-law's grandmother in Michigan lived very much like that not so long ago. She and her friends were very well dressed. They all lunched at their club, which was the social setting of their lives. It served not only a decorative function but also an existential one. The prominence of their husbands was marked by how they behaved, and families could rise and fall socially from one generation to the next according to these markers.

Even in the United States, supposedly a classless society, some people are more equal than others. You have that phrase "born on the wrong side of the tracks." Status is mostly established through women's assessments of each other. In many places, it is still the way in which the next generation gets married (or not) to the "right" people. It would make an interesting sociological study.

LA: That may be partly why my father was bothered that my mother wouldn't participate. She didn't allow him to show her off.

FG: Many times the social classification of families depends on their women's social skills. My father's best friend was a collateral descendant of the great nineteenth-century painter Chassériau. That family belonged to the gentry, but he felt he didn't have enough money to carry his title at the right level, so he dropped the "de."

What's more, his wife was absolutely not interested in any type of social activity. She was never happy with whatever house or apartment they lived in. They had beautiful canvases and furniture, but she wouldn't even unpack them most of the time, because she was already thinking about moving elsewhere. Intelligent, a rebel, she nevertheless smashed his career, because in France you must be convivial to survive.

LA: It's probably passive aggression, a woman's way of asserting herself.

FG: Either a woman is willing to play her part in the social fabric, or she isn't. It sounds as though your grandmother wanted to ameliorate the status quo and your mother wanted to diminish it. You came out of these contradictions wanting just to jump out altogether.

LA: Yes, like yourself. Wanting to get the hell out.

FG: That's interesting. Your grandmother dancing three steps forward, your mother doing two steps back, and you leaping forward into the unknown. *Reculer pour mieux sauter.*

LA: The result was that I didn't really feel part of that scene. My mother used to sing as a lullaby to all her babies a Yankee battle song that glorified Sherman's march through Georgia when he burned down Atlanta!

Yet looking back, I think, "God, not only were we part of that town; my grandparents were a founding family."

But I didn't perceive myself that way, so I moved north and became a resident of Vermont, where some of my mother's favorite ancestors lived and are buried.

FG: If you consider the times—the late 1950s—your grandmother's values certainly went against the grain of your own generation. Whereas in my own childhood my values were more in phase with those of my grandparents and not so much with my parents'. I identified with my grandparents.

LA: What were those values?

FG: I mean mostly my maternal grandparents. They were more relaxed and eccentric than my parents.

LA: Who were prisoners of convention?

FG: Yes, but at the same time, belonging to the intelligentsia, they were aware of contemporary trends in art and attended the best avant-garde plays. But they showed their feelings much less than my maternal grandparents.

LA: It sounds as though those grandparents had good senses of humor?

FG: My father also had an extremely good sense of humor, but it was always to put people down. He could kill with three words. Even his best friends disliked that about him. I found my parents more negative than my grandparents. Nothing was ever good enough. No one ever found grace in their eyes.

Whereas my grandparents weren't critical of other people, even when they didn't like them. They were a bit more innocent too. If my grandfather made jokes, they were never at someone else's expense. For instance, my grandfather would refer to my father's best friend, Mr. Chassériau, as Mr. Chamusot, Chapuso, Chaliso, et cetera, which exasperated my father. My grandfather loved to play with words, but my parents' generation thought there was nothing more vulgar than puns.

Also, my parents were a bit too much into dandyism, driven by a need to make life aesthetic at all times. To maintain an aesthetic stance in life, you don't have to engage emotionally. I preferred my grandparents' attitude of enthusiasm.

LA: But your grandmother was interested in making life more aesthetic, too, wasn't she?

FG: Yes, but she did it to make life more intense, not more aesthetic, which is a different thing. If she liked Isadora Duncan, it was because she developed a passionate interest in her dancing.

For my parents, even liking a painting was an intellectual exercise. My father thought you should be able to distinguish among great works of literature but without necessarily having to lead your life in accordance with their authors' beliefs.

My contention was that if you feel Rimbaud's poetry is good, you should live like Rimbaud. To my father, I was a barbarian. He felt a truly cultured person should know the difference between what you thought with your head, the aesthetic pleasure you derived from poetry, and how you shaped your own behavior. I felt your thoughts and actions had to be one.

LA: Making your thoughts and actions one is what the word "integrity" means.

FG: Yes, and my grandparents were of a generation in which they were all of a piece. My parents instead took a little of this and a little of that. If you like, they were more sophisticated. That's what they always resented about me, that coming from a sophisticated background, I behaved primitively!

They knew it was not an affectation, but they felt it was disagreeable of me to insist on being unconventional. I didn't want my actions to contradict my thoughts in any way. Which is very difficult, I must admit, now that I'm older. Now I am far from being entirely 100 percent that way, but when I was young, I really was.

One thing that annoyed me about my parents was that they could like this, that, and the other and understand it all. I said it was impossible. Their intellectual life was active, but it was the life of spectators. My approach was to be an actor in life, although I couldn't have put it into those words at that time.

Also, if someone gave me something I liked, I'd say, "It's so beautiful; I'm going to use it every day."

My mother would argue, "No, you should save it for special occasions. You're going to break it otherwise."

I'd say, "Possibly, but at least I will have used it to the utmost, and I will have experienced it in every circumstance until it's over."

My parents found this attitude barbaric and archaic. But I didn't like limitations or being sensible.

Apparently, some of my friends saw me as a bizarre creature, because they resembled my parents. Of course my style can lead to awkward situations. But at least that's what I wanted as a point of departure. I didn't want to spend my time being hypocritical.

LA: I've heard Eastern spiritual teachers say that they can't work with someone who has a bedside manner. Their minimum requirement is someone who's at least trying to operate from his or her authentic self.

FG: If you're already two-faced when you're young, what are you going to be like as an adult? Sometimes I was fairly demanding of my friends because I wanted them to have standards too. But probably they didn't even understand what I was talking about.

When you have to abide by what you express as your own beliefs, then you have to be more careful about what you say. That's why I think those Eastern teachers are right: you have to concentrate on what you can really hold on to.

LA: If the goal is to try to get in touch with your own core and you have all these layers of acts you're putting on, you confuse what's what.

FG: William Blake says something like, "He became what he envisioned." That's what I thought was important when I was young, to become what you intuit, not just to mix a little of this with a little of that. That's fine for everyday life, but it's not fine in terms of finding a direction for your development as a human being.

LA: I guess that attitude is based on the belief that a thought is an action. In other words, the word shapes the reality. So if you're talking garbage, you become a trash collector.

FG: Yes, I thought that if you have certain principles, you have to carry them to their natural consequences, rather than just maintaining them in a state of suspension.

That's why I was so pleased when I studied Indian philosophy, because it teaches that you must become one, that your thoughts, speech, and action must be harmonious and cut from whole cloth.

That explains why I could identify with someone like Pablo Picasso, who was forty years older than myself, close to the age of my grandmother. I identified with my grandparents' generation. Whereas you identified with your parents, especially with your mother, rather than with your grandmother. My children identified more with me than with my mother.

LA: I would say my daughter identifies with me, certainly more than with her grandparents.

FG: But her generation grew up in nuclear families, if that. Whereas you were in the same location as your parents and grandparents, and you could pick and choose whose values to adopt.

LA: I went home to Kingsport in 1980 with a friend who was the queen of the London leftists. She had magenta hair one week and turquoise the next, and women's symbol earrings. My grandmother took us to lunch at her country club. She turned to my friend and said, "Tell me, how is the servant problem in London these days?"

FG: Historical changes occur at different rates in different places. If you live in a big city, history is on fast rollers. But in the provinces of any given country, people have a more leisurely rhythm, and history is much slower.

LA: People refer to Appalachians as "our contemporary ancestors." And it's true. It's a different world.

FG: Yet they have a wealth of oral traditions, and much of the good country music comes from that region.

LA: Yes, there's a lot of creativity there. Someone said the South has produced so many fiction writers because it's the only part of the country where people can sit still long enough to write a novel.

FG: Also, you develop your imagination when you don't have an overload of material goods. Why should you imagine anything if you have everything? I didn't want my children to have too many toys because I think it annihilates the imagination.

When Paloma was a child, she was an excellent storyteller. Children would come to my home with her after school to listen to her intricate tales. She was possessed by the need to create her own world, not to accept a world created by somebody else, as on television.

My children went to the École Alsacienne, where it was forbidden that parents have a television their children could watch. So I had no television at all. If they wanted stories, I had to tell them one or they had to invent one, and they did.

When parents are too busy, instead of using the oral mode of communication, they give their children books or computer games. Now children of thirteen are communicating on the Internet with people they will never meet. It's a virtual reality that's slightly dangerous because, if infiltrated by fascist ideas, it could result in a complete generation indoctrinated the wrong way.

LA: If it's true that we create our own reality through the power of the imagination, how will such children be able to create their future reality?

FG: That impulse can be spent in ways that are not fruitful. Your grandmother had a fiction in her head, but she made it into a reality, which is the creative urge. God said, "Let there be light," and light was. Thinking, saying, or believing in something can make it happen. But if you're spending this energy in a kind of virtual reality, that becomes an end in itself.

So could you summarize the meaning for you of your Appalachian grandmother?

LA: It was her example as a strong woman that was most important for me, in contrast to my mother, who had her own kind of strength certainly but who was quiet and shy and bookish. Maybe my grandmother's club work seems superficial, but the effect of it on the town wasn't. They organized scholarships for deserving students who otherwise couldn't afford college. They were deciding the social pecking order of the town. My grandmother's function for me, though, was that of an example of a strong woman who was running everything in sight.

FG: She was a role model for you?

LA: Yes, and when her husband died, she grabbed my Latin teacher, and they went around the world twice on the *Queen Mary*. She took six major trips in the ten years after my grandfather died. I have photographs of her and my Latin teacher riding camels in front of the Pyramids. I also have photos of her in South America, India, Rome, all over the globe. She showed me that a woman can do whatever she decides to do.

FG: An American pioneer, a frontier woman.

LA: Yes. In a sense, she did what I later had to do in order to find myself: define myself as a writer, and then write. The odds against my ever getting published were staggering. I wrote fiction for fourteen years without getting published, and I collected 250 rejection slips. The stubbornness to stick with it came from her. She decided she

Elizabeth Vanover Reed (Lisa's paternal grandmother) and Grace Elmore (Lisa's Latin teacher) in Egypt during their round-the-world tour (1958).

was a southern lady, and, by God, she ended up a southern lady. I decided I was a writer, and I ended up a writer.

FG: A writer of fiction. When I write, I write nonfiction.

LA: But your life has been very dramatic, so you have only to record what actually happened. My life has been quite placid—eighteen years in small-town Tennessee, forty-five years in small-town Vermont. I wrote fiction partly to entertain myself.

In any case, reality seems to me a very dubious concept, and the border between fiction and nonfiction, permeable. My grandmother was acting her whole life, and none of us knew it. She deserves an Emmy.

FG: She was a product of her own imagination. She became what she dreamed.

LA: The South as a whole was an imaginary kingdom.

FG: That's why they're good writers. In philosophy, a difference is made between logos, the spoken or written word, and praxis, which is action. In Europe, it's well-known that when southern people have said something, they think it's done. In the North, they don't speak, but they do it. I can see that even in my son, who's half Spanish. When Claude has said something, he thinks it's done, but it's not done at all. That used to exasperate me when he was younger.

LA: Action begins with a thought. The thought determines the action.

FG: But northerners carry out the action without even thinking the thought. That's the interesting part. Goethe writes in *Faust*, "In the beginning was action." He wanted to depart from the notion "In the beginning was the word." Goethe's attitude is very Germanic and Anglo-Saxon. But your great writers in the United States tend to be from the South.

LA: It may be a question of climate. It's too hot in the South to do anything. You just sit and daydream and drink iced tea. I don't know what the arrival of air-conditioning is going to do to the southern literary tradition!

FG: In France, the great politicians were always from the South because they were good orators. They could grab their audience by the strength and persuasion of their speeches.

LA: That's true here, too.

FG: Even Hitler was a southerner, from Austria. You can't imagine someone from Hamburg being as hysterical as he was.

LA: The whole concept of the American South was imaginary. All this stuff about plantations. Over four million of the five and a half million "white" people in the South before the Civil War owned no slaves. Many in the mountains had never even seen one. Yet a quarter million men went to their deaths to preserve their right to own them. It was absurd.

FG: And seventy years later, this imaginary world was resurrected by Margaret Mitchell in *Gone with the Wind* and then resurrected again in the film of it. Even the least cultured people in Europe have read *Gone with the Wind*.

That, and *Moby-Dick*. They don't know anything else about the United States.

LA: One's the essence of New England, and the other is the essence of the Deep South.

FG: The painter Degas was from an aristocratic French-Italian family with a branch in New Orleans. He visited his cousins there when he was quite young, and one of his first masterpieces is a large composition displaying the activity at a cotton counter in their home-store with his cousins portrayed there.

There are many French families with branches in the South, and many Europeans feel an affinity for the South. Look how well Dixieland jazz was accepted by the French. Even the word "Dixie" comes from the French *dix,* used in some New Orleans parishes for the ten-dollar banknote.

I wonder if the early French settlers in America were not less racist than the settlers of English background. It is a well-known fact that they had an easy interaction with the different tribes they met as they traveled down the Mississippi all the way from Canada. In New Orleans, for instance, the Native Americans indicated to their French visitors where the highest ground was, the area least vulnerable to inundations from the gulf or the river. There, the French built Le Vieux Carré. This advice is still valid, and it protected the French Quarter during the flooding brought by Katrina.

But in more general terms, how did your Virginia grandmother influence you, vis-à-vis feminism?

LA: That was her feminism—deciding what she wanted to do and doing it and, in doing so, showing us all that it was possible.

FG: And also giving women a role to play in that little town. I assume they had discussions at their club meetings, so they worked to improve their minds?

LA: They wrote and delivered papers at many of their meetings. It was a combination of socializing and intellectual stimulation and good works. It was volunteerism.

FG: Volunteerism is an impressive feature of American life, which I noticed when I first started coming to the United States. In France, everything is organized by governmental agencies, so you have to enter a profession and do things through that channel. You cannot do things as a volunteer. That almost doesn't exist.

LA: Those ladies were constantly raising money for their projects. It might have been the only way many of them had any control over money, since the men usually handled the family finances.

FG: It might also have been a way to slip around the edges of their husbands' behavior, which was probably more cutthroat, with the workers on one side and the bosses on the other. Maybe the women with their volunteer work tried to make the social inequality less blatant and to amend the hardships their husbands were causing.

As a foreigner, I fell from my rocker when I saw so many women in the States doing really important things without being paid. I wondered, "What are they doing? If they want to become active, why don't they do it seriously?" Then, as I became more used to how this country works, I saw that it was quite a contribution.

LA: I had no idea volunteerism was uniquely American.

In our town, though, it was a class thing. Women worked in the mills and factories and as maids and on farms, but the wives of the managerial and professional classes didn't work outside their homes. So volunteerism was their work. And maybe it was, as you suggest, to counteract abuses perpetrated by their husbands.

FG: And to reestablish human values. That's not unimportant. It was an antidote to raw capitalism.

LA: It's still important in my hometown. This book festival I just attended was organized by several doctors' wives who don't have outside jobs but who thought, "If interesting things are going to happen around here, we have to make them happen." Volunteer work is part of the fabric of life in that town.

FG: And it's part of the fabric of the functioning of American democracy, so it's not unimportant.

LA: In high school, we all volunteered at the hospital. We were called candy stripers because of our pink-and-white-striped smocks. We also had social clubs and were constantly having car washes and bake sales to raise money.

FG: That still goes on even in New York. People raise money partying, walking in marathons, et cetera, for all kinds of causes.

LA: Sometimes those in my mother's generation and in my grandmother's belonged to the same clubs, so it was a way of bringing the different age-groups together. And our clubs in high school trained us to be club women when we

The 1802 farmhouse in Vermont where Lisa lived for thirty-two years and wrote her first five novels.

grew up, although I jumped the tracks. I put aside my Scarlett O'Hara gown and went to college in Massachusetts. Then I moved to Vermont and rarely went home—until more recent years, in which I've spent a lot of time in East Tennessee and really grown to appreciate my homeland.

3. LA GUERRE EN DENTELLE

LA: You've suggested that the war between the sexes is not so intense in France as in the United States. What form does it assume there?

FG: There's more give-and-take. It's *la guerre en dentelle*, the war in lace. In the seventeenth century, men of the aristocracy would go to war, but they had those beautiful lace cuffs, so they were fighting the war but watching not to damage their lace.

Back to the war of the sexes, a man might want to conquer a woman, but he will do that by pretending to be altogether devoted, by sending flowers or small presents every day. Men are supposed to be chivalrous to women, so aggressive remarks are veiled in wit and compliments.

In Spain, this exchange can take other forms like *piropo* in Madrid. People walk on the mall, the young men walking together and the young women walking together. As they pass each other, the men say things that are courteous and a little bit risqué, somewhat arrogant and impudent. The women put them in their place by answering with a brief and witty rebuttal.

This kind of exchange exists in France also, but it's not as ritualized. It's a tension, but at the same time it's very playful, and it allows someone to see how worthy and intelligent the other one is without having to go steady and all that. It's courtship codified through language, so it doesn't come to blows and bruises.

Since I am French, something that shocks me in the United States is when a man says to someone, "You look beautiful today," and that person answers, "Thank you." In France, we never say thank you to a compliment. It would mean you don't accept it.

LA: Here it's considered rude not to say thank you. A friend of mine has a two-and-a-half-year-old grandson who goes to nursery school in California. One item on their list of activities for his age-group is instruction in the art of saying "please" and "thank you." So he races around his parents' house yelling "please" and "thank you" constantly, and in completely inappropriate situations. Americans, and especially southerners, are like parrots when it comes to those words. Someone who doesn't say them at the required moments is in danger of social ostracism.

FG: In France, it's considered extremely impolite to say thank you. It shows you have no imagination from the *piropo* point of view. Yet if you don't respond at all, as if you heard nothing, and refer instead to the weather, for example, it shows you don't accept the compliment at all. You're sending it back without being rude.

Conversely, if you accept it, you can say something like, "I thought that perhaps you would like this dress." Or, "Yes, I cut my hair in a different manner." You simply agree with the person who offered the compliment. If I tell you that your eyes look as blue as your lavender shirt and you reply, "Thank you," I am left out in the cold.

LA: For me, it would be almost impossible not to say thank you. I'm like one of Pavlov's dogs trained to salivate upon hearing a bell. I automatically say thank you whenever I receive a compliment or experience a kindness. It's like a Tourette's tic with me. I'm sure it must be very annoying for those around me who aren't southern!

FG: Since I've been living in this country for almost fifty years, I even catch myself saying thank you now and then. And I have to pray that it doesn't happen when I'm in France!

In England, people say "sorry" all the time. In France, you aren't supposed to excuse yourself. My mother taught me, "Don't do a silly thing, but if you have, don't excuse yourself. It's bad form."

I had a tendency to say, "I didn't do it on purpose."

And my mother would reply, "Of course not. I hope not. If on top of it all, you'd done it on purpose, this would really be too much! If you know it's bad, then don't do it. Otherwise, don't bother me with your excuses."

These are cultural habits that you can't know about in a foreign country unless someone there explains them to you.

One time I was packing to go to the United States and a friend came over. I showed him my brand-new leather suitcase and said, "I'm so glad I've coordinated my shoes, purses, et cetera. Everything is black and white."

And he said, "Isn't it a pity? Beautiful as you are, these are the only two colors that don't suit you." That's a typical French joke, one that hides a compliment.

LA: In other words, he preferred to make the joke rather than to pat you on the back?

FG: Right. Anybody could have said, "Oh, that's marvelous." Many French people use their senses of humor for and against one another. In *la guerre en dentelle,* you say very satirical things or incredible compliments; both must be exaggerated, so you know not to take it too seriously.

For example, apart from my father, most Frenchmen don't like the color pure white. So if you're wearing white, a man might tell you, "You're dressed as if you were a beautiful water lily tonight. Except that this pond isn't the pond for it." In other words, a compliment and a hidden snake in the grass: he found you overdressed for the occasion.

LA: When I was first spending time in Paris, I met an American woman who was working there and who had several American women friends also working there. They met regularly to give each other moral support, and she talked about their disgust over the floridness of Frenchmen's compliments. She said, "I can't believe that stuff actually works." But I guess those compliments aren't meant to "work"; they're just meant for fun, to make everyone feel good?

FG: When a woman walks in the street in Paris, men in a truck or a car are entitled to whistle or to make a remark as they pass by. It's not meant to lead anywhere. American friends sometimes say, "I was attacked in the street today." By which they mean that some man said something to them in passing.

I reply, "Well, they were trying to pay you a compliment. But since you aren't used to it, you jump to conclusions."

LA: When it happens here, it's often an insult.

FG: In Paris, a woman will say, "Today in the street I heard three whistles and four comments. I don't need my mirror to know I'm in good shape."

Hearing what the people say is hearing the voice of God. It enhances self-confidence. Frenchwomen consider that a plus.

LA: Women here resent being turned into an object, knowing that any clod on the street can assess them physically or sexually, often in unflattering terms.

FG: But since in France it's a flattering remark and it's not going to be an attack of any kind, it will just reinforce your knowledge that you're beautiful. During a day, if I hear several pleasant comments on my appearance, I find that encouraging.

LA: There's so much violence against women here, and women feel it sets the climate for men's violating their personal space.

FG: There are probably fewer rapes in France because people are less repressed. If a man whistles at you and you smile, that oils the social wheels and eases the tension between the classes and sexes. It affirms that you both belong to the same culture. It's a kind of give-and-take that acknowledges that the other person exists, so in that sense it's not treating another person as an object.

To take offense all the time makes every relationship disagreeable or combative. Each time a man says something to me, if I take it as an insult, then I'll be insulted several times a day by strangers I'll never see again. Whereas if I smile vaguely and go my way, it doesn't cost me very much. It's a fact that the French try to avoid sharp corners within genders and among the different layers of society. We believe that it's part of the democratic spirit that any man of any station has a right to find a woman beautiful and to express it, even if he knows full well he'll never get to know her. And she has to have the ease to be gracious. It has to do with equality and with giving and receiving a moment of joy.

In New York, people don't look at each other, and since I'm French, I have a tendency to look at people. If they look at me, I have a vague smile, and they know perfectly well that I have nothing in mind other than not wanting to meet their gaze without acknowledging it.

Something I don't like in the United States is that people enter a taxi without greeting the driver before saying where they want to go. I always say, "Good morning," or whatever, and they are always so surprised because nobody ever says that to them. It's not that I'm trying to get them to notice me as a woman or anything else. I'm simply being polite, acknowledging their presence as human beings, not just taxi drivers.

LA: Well, I do that too. But both Paris and the American South are what the anthropologist Edward T. Hall calls "high-context cultures." In such cultures, you may know many of the people with whom you interact during a day, or your family does, in one context or another. (In the South, you're often related to them!) So polite individual interactions are important in a way that they aren't in more anonymous "low-context cultures" like New York City.

FG: Those little exchanges are harmless, they don't hurt anyone, so why shouldn't we make the effort?

LA: Well, there may be a difference in the kinds of comments that are made in the United States and France.

FG: You're right. Here it's four-letter words. In Europe, it's never an overt sexual comment; it's simply a compliment. In France, we don't have four-letter words; we have three-letter words and five-letter words! But you don't hear those on the street, unless you're driving a car and cut off another driver and he uses one of them on you. But if he wants to annoy you, he will usually use words like "potato" or "sausage." The worst insult is "little mother," which means he finds you neither a good driver nor an attractive person!

LA: You say that in *la guerre en dentelle* women don't ever say no to men directly because they can convey the refusal in ways that allow men to keep their pride intact?

FG: When I was fifteen, a number of young men started noticing me, so I asked my father how to get rid of them. I didn't want to say no from fear of being impolite, but I didn't want to say yes.

"Of course not," said my father. "But I thought you were a woman?"

Meaning that I had to have the guile to find ways to refuse without saying no. Right away, I started to think about what those means were, and I realized there were several ways to let the advance go by without having to issue a clear no and of course without saying yes.

Displacing the focus of attention is a good one. For example, if the young man were rather proud of himself, you began by flattering him, praising him to the skies: "You're so marvelous, you're so this, you're so that." And then he forgot what he was after.

Once I had to use a similar strategy on someone from whom I needed help in a legal situation. I went to see him at his office in late afternoon without a clue that he had anything else on his mind. He got up from his desk and came toward me with clear intentions. On the one hand, I was appalled. On the other, I had to think fast. So right off, I turned away from him and admired a painting on the wall as if I hadn't seen his movement.

LA: And he realized you weren't interested?

FG: No, he didn't realize anything, but he couldn't state his next sentence. He was deterred for a few minutes while we discussed the painting. Then he had to go back and sit at his desk because my attitude was so unencouraging.

Then he said, "Well, if you want me to do such and such, you should come to my apartment next Friday, et cetera."

I performed the second act, which was to pay exaggerated compliments, murmuring, "Well, of course, I admire your skill and intelligence, et cetera, et cetera."

I buttered him up for about ten minutes. Then I added that I wasn't free Friday so what about the following Wednesday, but anyway the legal matter had to be settled before that date.

Since I'd paid him all those compliments, he thought he had won the case, forgetting I was also a lawyer. So we agreed to meet the following Wednesday. Meanwhile, he signed what I needed him to sign.

On the Wednesday, I called him feigning a cold, saying I was extremely ill with a temperature, so I had to postpone.

A few days later, he called to find out when we could see each other, and I said, "In the meantime, I've been through the most terrible moral dilemma when I think about my friend so-and-so with whom you're having a relationship. How could I do that to her? I must have lost my mind the previous week because I admire you and you're so exceptional, but now I see clearly how impossible it is."

So that was it, and he wasn't even angry with me. It's part of the human comedy. I paved the way with so many compliments that he ended up feeling like a peacock. I had the grace to lead him on. Which means that I paid attention to him and worked through all those complications!

He said, "Well, I see you got what you wanted." And he admired my skill for doing so.

LA: And he got to feel like a rake.

FG: Yes, and he had no reason to doubt that I was really ill or that I was having all those guilt feelings. He certainly had done this many other times with other women. But it was inappropriate to try it with me since I was a friend of the woman in his life. So I had no intention of letting anything happen. Of course it's more convenient here, where you just say no and blast it all and you don't care.

But is it so important actually to consummate a seduction, or is it only important to have reached the point at which you know quite well that had you added some more tender words, you could have achieved your goal? Is it necessary to go that far, since you have already succeeded in making someone desire you, yet you don't really care for the result?

{ 106 }

This game can be considered very empty when seen from abroad. People outside France think that the French are the best at indoor sports. Maybe in a way it's true, but some of the best indoor sports are simply conversation and some of the intricacies that go on between people trying to seduce each other without necessarily wanting the ultimate act. The game of seduction has already been done so many times by so many people, including ourselves, so why should we pursue it indefinitely?

The interest lies more often in the early stages of a conquest. That's what people really enjoy. They find the most tremendous gratification, even erotic pleasure, from experiencing whether seduction is possible or not. But once they find that it is, remembering that there is work to be done tomorrow morning, why insist on lovemaking, unless there is a stronger and deeper attraction?

Virginia Woolf says it best, as usual: "Yet this showing off, which is not copulating, necessarily, nor altogether being in love, is one of the great delights, one of the chief necessities of life. Only then does all effort cease; one ceases to be honest, one ceases to be clever. One fizzes up into some absurd delightful effervescence of soda water or champagne through which one sees the world tinged with all the colours of the rainbow."

All this originated in *l'amour courtois*, the courtly love of the troubadours in the thirteenth century. The verb "to flirt" comes from *conter fleurette* (literally, "to tell a floweret"; in other words, "to whisper sweet nothings"). It was an end in itself, assessing a potentiality, not a fact.

LA: Well, that's a big cultural difference, because I would say that in America people actually like the physical sensations of lovemaking. I mean, the seduction is conducted in order to have those sensations. The attitude you describe is similar to the idea in France of having all this beautiful food around that you can look at and smell but not eat. It's the same principle that governs the striptease!

FG: When I came to the United States for the first time in 1961, I met Diana Vreeland from *Vogue* at the Oak Room. I was having lunch with her and a friend of mine from Poland. Both of them ordered a lot of different dishes, and I was astonished, because they were both very thin. When the food appeared, they just toyed with the items on their plates, sniffing the aroma.

And as the untouched food was carried away, Diana said, "Oh, what a nice memory."

She was the czar of fashion, and as such she didn't eat at all. She was American, but her attitude was absolutely French: to be surrounded by beautiful things but not to partake.

LA: But your friend was from Poland, and Diana Vreeland was from another planet! And New York is an international city, not an American one. I assure you that abstention is not the norm in America. Down on the farm, whether it's in Tennessee or Vermont, people enjoy the physical act of lovemaking more than any mind games that might precede it.

This may say something very interesting about which senses are developed in the different cultures—the sense of touch in ours, the sense of sight in yours. And I acknowledge that the sense of touch is the most primitive in the hierarchy of the senses. But if the idea in fashion in France is, as you've said, to conceal your defects and reveal your assets, when you actually go to bed with people and you're naked with them, they see all the defects.

FG: Not always. A bedroom may be more flattering than a living room, depending on the light! But sometimes, it's true, ultimate revelations may be shattering.

LA: And the illusion can be destroyed. And everybody's disappointed. Whereas if you just walk away, the other person can live forever with the illusion of what might have been?

FG: I agree. Eroticism is all in the imagination anyway.

LA: But it seems to me that by turning lovemaking into a game of hide-and-seek, you never get to know the other person. It takes time and trust for two people to reveal themselves to each other, with all their hopes and fears and vulnerabilities. I think that's the kind of connection many people in this country are looking for. And if that bond is established, lovemaking becomes a way to honor and reinforce it, kind of like Holy Communion for a Christian. But different cultures have different attitudes, and I guess in France sex is regarded as a sport rather than a sacrament?

FG: Well, those whistles and comments to women in the street in France have a function, and that function is to make the whole atmosphere more sexually charged. It's like a garden in which there are many flowers, each giving off its own perfume. It's heady. As the day goes by and the evening lingers, you're more likely to say yes rather than no to your lover.

I'd characterize French culture as love oriented, in the general sense of the word. Everyone contributes his little part, even if he or she doesn't get specific satisfaction from it. In that sense, I'm not a feminist, because insisting on being ethical and whatnot makes a culture extremely trivial, pragmatic, and boring.

When I'm in the United States, I rarely feel very sexual because the culture itself isn't sexual, so I can forget about that very easily. Here everyone talks about having sex. In France, there's not even a way to say that: "J'ai fait le sexe avec quelqu'un." It's not even grammatical. "J'ai fait l'amour." "I made love."

LA: It may simply be the difference between a more ancient, jaded culture and a young, hyperactive one. Many Americans spend a lot of energy trying to damp down their eroticism so that it doesn't dominate their lives. Most people I know don't need the efforts of an entire culture to turn them on, since they're turned on much of the time anyway, by the flow of the life force through their bodies.

Also, I'm not sure I see the point in heating up the oven if you don't intend to cook a meal. It seems cruel to those who are starving, rubbing their noses in what they can't have.

And what about the French word *baiser*, which I understand in vulgar usage means "to fuck"?

FG: The word means a kiss, and the verb means "to embrace." It comes from the Middle Ages, and it's more erotic than pornographic.

There's always a subtle ambience of eroticism in the streets, in the air, of Paris. For instance, when you go to the market to select peaches, if you ask the vendor, "Are your peaches ripe?" he'll often say yes with a wink because the peach is considered a fruit similar to the female sex. Sometimes having intercourse is referred to as "eating a peach." So there will often be a little innuendo that isn't rude but just reminds you of the eroticism of life. Yet you can buy as many pounds of peaches as you wish without anything happening at all. Grown-up people don't have to behave like prigs.

LA: I think women react badly to comments in the street here because they're often delivered with the intention of demeaning.

FG: Either that or they're imagining that that's the intention. *Le pire n'est pas toujours sûr.* The worst is not always certain. So why should you think the worst of somebody when you are not sure this is what he meant. By assuming it's meant well and not intended to be nasty, I teach something.

LA: I tend to cringe when I hear a comment in the street. I'll give you an example. I was in San Francisco on a book tour. I was staying in a hotel downtown, and I went out very early one morning to buy some shampoo. As this man in a business suit passed me, he said, "Well, there goes another dyke looking for some pussy to suck."

FG: I never heard anything like that in France. People are probably less angry there.

LA: Many women here have similar stories—to say nothing of the 20 percent who've experienced sexual assault. It's about twice the French rate, I think.

FG: That means this culture is very violent. No one wants to see the comic aspect of things. You could also have made a simple gesture implying that the man was impotent or given him "the chicken look" from feet to head and back again, and he would have tripped on the sidewalk.

LA: I've always been taught not to engage with the insane. I just assumed that his wife had run off with another woman, so he was taking it out on me.

FG: My conclusion would be that this society is neo-puritanical. This explains all the S/M and the violent desire to punish or be punished. And late-night television is often real pornography. It's a neo-puritanical attitude that sex has to be obscene, dirty, et cetera. Men here must be dissatisfied because they aren't getting what they want sexually, so there's much more hatred between the sexes. So men go to extremes.

I don't have that type of thing in my experience. I've been attacked in the street in Albuquerque, but just to be robbed. It's very unpleasant. I've never been attacked in France, but that doesn't mean a thing, because it still could happen.

But by and large, it seems that everybody's attitude here has engendered bad will. The aggressive mood seems to be in the ascendant here. It's more fight than flight. Because the French have twenty-five hundred years of history behind them and have seen so many fights, maybe we have a tendency to take things more lightly.

LA: I do like this idea that an entire culture might conspire to try to lend a little champagne to life. That's lovely.

FG: On the fourteenth of July in towns and villages all over France, they build a wooden dance floor in the village center and hire an orchestra, and people dance all night under lanterns. A bit of rejoicing for people of all ages. They get dressed to the nines, often coming there with something erotic in mind.

You dance with your own partner; you dance with several if you're on the prowl. Then fireworks. Everyone in town goes because you get such a marvelous feeling, reduced to the most youthful part of yourself. It's very erotic in general. There's something in the air. Being together multiplies individual impulses. It conspires toward erotic resolution. Here there is mostly anger in the air.

LA: But this is such a multicultural society.

FG: Ah, look, in France now . . .

LA: In France now, there's not a lot of affection from the French toward the North Africans, for example, or vice versa.

FG: That's true. There are altercations and worse . . . There are blood crimes committed for either racial, religious, or political reasons. There is a surge of hatred caused, in part, by non-assimilation to a culture based on democratic freedom and dialogues between opposed metaphysical concepts.

LA: Here the entire culture is mixed. So it's no wonder that people are at each other's throats, because they've left behind their cultures of origin and they don't know who they are. But to return to the theme of eroticism, the

French seem more androgynous than many other Europeans, yet it's in France where everybody is always talking about "vive la différence." The assumption there seems to be that men and women are essentially different, whereas in the United States the assumption is that gender differences are, to some extent, merely conditioned by society. Do the French stress the differences so insistently because they're in doubt about them?

FG: Frenchwomen like to be as seductive as possible. That doesn't mean that they're expecting to have more affairs than women in this country. But they want in their manners to affirm that they're women.

Of course in France, women tread on the high side of the sidewalk. They must be beautiful enough or smart enough, chic enough or intelligent enough to stand their higher ground vis-à-vis men. You position yourself as a goddess, and if you are successful, men are subservient to you, they are your supplicants. Of course they are at the same time trying to conquer you and reverse the order of things.

French men and women, even though they may be rather androgynous, accentuate the appearance of being male and female. But it's mostly a mating behavior, like the peacock with his sublime plumage. Do they really want to mate? Not all that much most of the time. It's a form of social interplay, the multicolored rainbow of desire.

If someone comes to my studio and finds me in my blue jeans and an old sweater working at my paintings, I'm not at my best. I can't possibly go out to dinner like that. I'll attempt to present myself in a more elaborate aspect of my persona so as to play my part in the social comedy. If

I'm tired and my hair is a mess and I haven't paid attention to what I'm wearing, I'd be an impediment to the evening. I'm not bringing champagne, I'm bringing water, and to top it all it's tepid. If I behave that way consistently, even my friends will find me a bore because I've become a nuisance, not a contributor.

It's basically the same in New York. When people invite me, they expect me to bring a little bit of wit and elegance; otherwise they wouldn't invite me. There are people who say, "You must love me as I am." Then they look awful and are boring. They might have more friends if they made some effort.

LA: But the business of playing up your femaleness . . .

FG: But I can't play up my maleness, because I'm female. I can play up my androgyny because I have the brain of a male. But I can't play up my male side, because I'm not a male.

LA: But you could play up neither. Frenchwomen are more female in their presentation than women in other Western countries. Think about most British women or Danish women.

FG: That's true. During the day the differences aren't so great, but during the evening, yes. For one thing, all business talk is suspended in France. The men don't gravitate to one side of the room and the women to the other. You're supposed to have a general conversation, and everyone is meant to try to be witty, interesting, agreeable, and to embody the other side of life.

In France, we work during the day just to be able to

enjoy a pleasant evening. Here people work during the day in order to become rich or to be efficient. I admire Anglo-Saxon society because it's very utilitarian and pragmatic, and most of the time I don't want to be encumbered with all those graces. But if you ask me where the graces are, they are in the other attitude. But to have the other attitude, you must be ready to waste a lot of time.

4. FIVE GENERATIONS
OF WOMEN

FG: Women who have children want to educate them and prepare them for life. They certainly don't neglect the rational aspect of knowledge, but they also want to transmit a more ancient treasure trove of lore and customs. For this, they enchant young minds with fanciful tales. Most women of the previous generations whom I knew were excellent storytellers. Thanks to oral tradition, patterns of speech and modes of expression are passed on, as well as historical and mythical material.

When I was growing up, not only did the women tell me stories in the evening, like "Hop o' My Thumb" and "Little Red Riding Hood" and the Perrault, Andersen, and Grimm tales, they also retold the past, as they had experienced it or heard about it. And they wove the yarn of their sentences with care, in the same way in which they took pride in writing beautiful letters.

One can see families in which this tradition does not exist and how little their offspring know about writing essays or expressing themselves fluently in speech. Even with a busy professional life, I purposefully told a lot of stories to my children. I am glad to see that they all express themselves well orally and can also write easily, this having nothing to do with what they learned at school.

The oral transmission of history and values is like the milk the mother gives the infant, which both nurtures and conveys immunities. It's really a very intimate process. "The milk of human kindness" is the best guarantee against boorishness, violence, and nihilism. It remains a safeguard of civilization.

LA: One thing that surprised me in Paris is how well everybody tells stories. In that sense, it reminds me a lot of the American South. I hadn't known that was an important part of French culture. Sitting around a dinner table, people compete with each other to tell the best stories.

FG: Quite so. At times, it's not the story itself that is so important but the way words are used to bring it to life.

Letter writing is also taught by French mothers and grandmothers to their children. My mother and my maternal grandmother were extremely good epistolarians. Apart from letters to family and friends, they also had to write letters to people not their intimate friends on formal occasions such as weddings and funerals.

My mother and grandmother liked to specialize in happy events and discovered, to their delight, that I was rather gifted for the sad ones. So when I reached eight years of age, they would ask me to put myself in the proper mood because so-and-so had died. And I would draft a model for the letter of condolence that they could copy, if they liked it, or improve upon if necessary.

I found many ways to say how we shared their grief, and how we loved the person they had lost, and all the compassion we felt. I loved these unfortunate tidings, and like an actress I truly experienced what it would be like if, being a grown-up, I had lost my husband or my son.

So the letter was not an unfeeling type of polite condolence. I made it much more dramatic and attempted to share in their actual grief. I absolutely adored it and was pleased when my mother or grandmother used what I had concocted.

LA: Would you read books for inspiration?

FG: No. Putting myself in the given situation, I became quite bereaved. I would even cry. After shedding my tears, I would blow my nose and write the letter. Then my mother or grandmother would say, "This is a pretty good one." Or, "No, there's one sentence too much here." After editing, they would copy it and send it.

It was a boon to my embryonic pride, and I usually got some pocket money for the movies or to go ice-skating. I believe they were unaware that as I was already high-strung, such an exercise was perhaps not excellent for my nerves. They just enjoyed the precocious maturity of my official style.

LA: At least they paid you!

FG: They had no obligation to, but there had to be some encouragement. Then if I produced a really fine one, they would keep it as a model for all similar circumstances.

LA: That is hysterical!

FG: Yes, come to think of it, it makes me laugh! I also believe that my father and my paternal grandmother would have been utterly shocked to know about such an exploitation of my literary abilities! It did add fuel to my natural tendency to pathos.

LA: In the South, we got training in the art of the thank-you note. At Christmas, some mothers wouldn't let their children open their next gift until they'd written a thank-you note for the previous one. Every time I went someplace or received a present, my mother would chain me to my desk with a card and pen. She was a virtuoso at the thank-you note. By the time she got through with you, you felt that your house she'd just visited was Shangri-La or that the gift you'd given her was the Hope Diamond—even if she'd already returned it for a refund.

Pat Nixon once said that as First Lady she would get on an airplane and write thank-you notes to everybody who had just entertained her. She was quoted as saying, "No one escapes without a thank-you note."

FG: For me, the memory of writing those kinds of notes is linked to the way in which women exorcised violence by including in everyday life all the social aspects of culture, including activities related to fashion and the applied arts, like ceramics, bookbinding, and other handicrafts. After World War I, Frenchwomen thought that if they couldn't compete with men in Art, with a capital A, they could at least survive financially through entering such professions.

Around 1928, a well-known department store, Le Printemps, initiated a new section called Primavera. The woman who headed that department was given free rein to select whatever items she wanted in the brand-new Art Deco style: ceramics, majolica, and other objects. After 1929, when the Depression started, many women who had not needed to work before began to earn their keep via this activity.

In the context of the economic liberation of women in France, much importance was given to applied arts. It became a channel much broader than that for fine arts— not that there were not already some well-known women painters such as Suzanne Valadon and Marie Laurencin. Most women thought that working in applied arts made less strife within their families. Nobody objected to a woman's becoming skilled in such ventures. Whereas relatives might still be objecting to a woman's becoming an artist and joining bohemian circles.

LA: Because it was considered that decorating homes was a more feminine activity?

FG: Probably, and since this step forward happened thanks to women of my mother's generation, I got to know quite a few of them, including one called Paule Marrot, who started hand painting motifs on chintz-like fabrics that were then used for curtains and upholstery. Everybody in Paris who was *somebody* had to have fabrics by Paule Marrot.

Chintz is made of linen or cotton, and once painted or printed, it's varnished or iced. Once iced, it's called glacé, and it looks very pretty indeed. Most of Paule Marrot's designs had a white background, and then in free style she painted very imaginative floral combinations or whatever she thought appropriate to harmonize her subjects and colors with the style of the room.

She became extremely successful. Her clientele mostly belonged to the intellectual bourgeoisie, women and men who were a bit artistic. Her fabrics became a craze, a status symbol. Everyone had to have her creations. To this day, there is still a shop selling her designs, which are now printed in larger quantities and still bear her name and signature.

Another interesting aspect of that surge of female creativity between the two world wars had to do with the influx and input of the White Russian immigrants from Moscow and St. Petersburg, who brought to Paris their folkloric traditions, their zest for life, their modern ideas, and the urgent need to make a living. My grandmother befriended some Russian women and learned to decorate blouses and dresses with *point de croix* embroidery in different colors.

Many of these new Paris residents became well-known, such as Lola Prusac. The most illustrious, Sonia Delaunay, was an excellent painter, but she was also a dress designer and a trendsetter. She even created color-coordinated cars that matched women's outfits. There would have been no Art Deco movement without women artists like Sonia Delaunay, Tamara de Lempicka, or the Groult sisters, interior decorator friends of Marie Laurencin's.

Everything my mother liked loomed big in my imagination as a young child. I thought, "How marvelous, there is a woman who can make drapes and curtains!" My ambitions were still timid, but I thought for sure I could do some kind of applied art. My ultimate goal was painting, of course, but I was secure in the thought that the field of applied arts was open to me.

This is just to say that it takes more than one generation for people to have the courage to confront the altogether unknown. Creativity doesn't just surge out of the blue. In your case, for example, maybe your mother, whether she knew it or not, wanted to become a writer, so then you became one.

LA: That's possible. Originally, she wanted to be a nurse, but her father thought that life would be too grueling for her, so she married a doctor and lived out her medical ambitions through him. She became a high school English teacher while my father was finishing medical school. But she hated the job because her students were almost as old as she, and many of the boys were much taller. She had a hard time maintaining discipline.

Books were very important around our house. My mother read constantly, often a book a day. Books were her drug of choice. She read to us children every night. Though my father said one night he came home and found her reading to us from the adult book she'd been reading herself during that day! She also took us to the library every week, where our names were entered on a chart. We got gold and silver stars and bird stickers according to how many books we read.

When I was away from home, at summer camp or later at college, my mother wrote a long letter every week. My friends adored her letters because they were so well written and witty. So it's possible that by becoming a professional writer, I was trying to fulfill my mother's thwarted literary ambitions. Also, I might have realized that saying something in a book was the only way to get her attention. Do you think you were fulfilling your mother's repressed wish to be an artist?

FG: I believe so, even though nobody except herself was preventing my mother from continuing to create. My grandmother was also gifted and skillful. For the family, she made purses and hats that were very fashionable, similar to ones sold at Chanel.

In France, my generation was already the third generation of professional women. Whereas it seems to me that in the United States yours is the second generation of professional women.

LA: I would say that for the South, I'm the first generation. Speaking, of course, only of upper-middle-class white women. Black women always worked, some as slaves before the Civil War and then as maids and cooks. Working-class women worked in factories and mills. Farm wives worked for survival from dawn to midnight. Even plantation wives apparently worked very hard, despite what *Gone with the Wind* portrays. Recent scholarship itemizes their overwhelming responsibilities, raising their many children and managing their servants and households.

There's a contradiction between the stereotype of the flighty, flirtatious southern belle and the all-nurturing matriarch she was supposed to become immediately after marriage. The idle southern lady is largely a myth, but insofar as it existed, it was upper-middle-class white women living in towns who had the leisure to concern themselves with manners, graces, and their appearances.

The situation was somewhat different in the North, though. My great-grandmother Ruth Maria Griswold Green Pealer was first married to a miller from Germany. He died from Bright's disease when my grandfather was five. To support herself and her son, she became a piano teacher. But then she remarried and moved to Washington, D.C., where she worked as a journalist and as a staff genealogist for the Daughters of the American Revolution, a paid position.

She was a distant cousin of Elizabeth Cady Stanton, the leader, along with Susan B. Anthony, of the first wave of suffragists from 1850 until the early twentieth century.

FG: Around what year did she go to Washington?

LA: Eighteen ninety-six. While she was still living in up-

Ruth Maria Griswold Green Pealer, Lisa's suffragist great-grandmother (ca. 1897).

state New York, she was a local organizer for suffrage and an official in the Woman's Christian Temperance Union. She gave speeches to local groups about women's rights and about the abuse of women and children by drunken men. The WCTU wasn't so much opposed to alcohol as to the brutality unleashed by those who drank it, so the battered women's movement is nothing new.

She decided she needed to be where the action was. My grandfather quoted her as saying about her little town in upstate New York, "If I don't get out of here, I'll go crazy." She hated housework and insisted that she and her husband live in a hotel in Washington, where someone else would make the beds and cook their meals.

In addition to her journalism, her work for women's rights, and her various genealogical groups, she was secretary-general for the United Spanish War Veterans and Women's Auxiliary, president and treasurer for the Women's National Press Association, and a member of United States Daughters of 1812, the Order of the Eastern Star, and the Order of Patrons of Husbandry. So she was a very busy girl.

The goal of Elizabeth Cady Stanton and Susan B. Anthony was to get each state to pass an amendment allowing women the vote. They got four states during their lifetimes—Wyoming, Colorado, Idaho, Utah. Women on the frontier had proven themselves equal to men in terms of hard work and courage.

FG: Also there were not that many women out there, and men did whatever the women wanted to encourage them to stay. You see that even in the western movies. The towns were entirely male, and when a few women arrived, men were enchanted and wanted to please them.

LA: Also, it wasn't any real threat to the men, since there were so few women. Their votes couldn't swing an election.

FG: Yes, when women rank as a minority, men let them do what they want, as a token of male generosity unlikely to alter the response to any serious issue.

LA: My great-grandmother was part of the third generation of the first-wave American feminists. In 1920, an amendment to the national constitution was finally ratified by the necessary three-fourths of the states—thirty-six, in other words. Sadly, this was after my great-grandmother died.

The thirty-sixth state was Tennessee. The vote looked very close, and organizers pro and con spent a lot of time and money in Nashville lobbying the legislators. It looked as though the suffragists were going to lose by one vote.

During the voice vote, a representative from east Tennessee, my home region, a young man of twenty-four who everyone thought was opposed to the amendment, voted for it. So the bill passed both in Tennessee and in the nation as a whole.

The opponents were so enraged that the young legislator had to climb out a window and hide in an attic. Somebody asked him later why he changed his vote, and he said the previous night he'd received a letter from his mother in the mountains saying, "Be a good boy, and do the right thing."

What interests me most is that it took nearly three generations to accomplish this, seventy years.

My other maternal great-grandmother raised championship Buff Plymouth Rock chickens in partnership with her son, which they showed and sold for breeding purposes. They also judged poultry competitions nationally. Her daughter, my maternal grandmother, worked as a secretary for an incubator company before her marriage.

After their marriage, my maternal grandmother and grandfather moved to West Ninety-Third Street in New York City, where he worked as a lawyer for the Erie Railroad. He used to tell about coming home and finding his wife in tears because she had no work, no friends, no income, nothing to do.

That idleness didn't last long, as she soon had five daughters. Each of my grandmother's daughters, my aunts, worked before marriage—my mother as a teacher, the others as secretaries. One aunt continued to work as society editor for the *Los Angeles Times* after she married. Another taught high school Latin.

My grandfather insisted his daughters have careers by which they could support themselves if they had to. But he didn't necessarily let them follow their inclinations: my aunt Mary wanted to be a lawyer, but he himself found law boring and wouldn't allow it.

In his practice, he saw many women in bad marriages from which they couldn't escape because they couldn't support themselves and their children, so he gave each of his daughters a sum of money to be put away in case they needed to leave their husbands, the implications of which must not have endeared him to his sons-in-law.

FG: Being able to stand on your own two feet is an attitude more typical of northern countries. My family is from northern France, but my friend Geneviève from Languedoc wasn't expected to work ever. She could hardly put one foot in front of the other! She didn't work well at school. Why should she? It wasn't expected of her.

LA: She probably had the same experience I did at Wellesley of coming to your school and not having a clue what was going on. But she apparently didn't feel as challenged by it as I did.

FG: In my class at school was another girl from the same region who was very bright and who worked hard. Not that Geneviève wasn't bright, but she was extremely lazy.

LA: It may simply be a question of what a culture values. Northern cultures value activity, whereas southern cultures value leisure and style.

FG: When the climate is cold, you have to activate yourself.

LA: To survive. To build a house, gather and preserve food, provide heat.

FG: So you're of my children's generation, and you're the first generation of professional women in the South. Whereas in France I'm of your mother's generation, and I'm the third generation of professional women. We got the vote much later, but the professionalism came earlier. Different phases happen at different rates in the different countries.

LA: Why didn't your mother work?

FG: My mother was mostly an artist, and she continued her ceramics for a few years after her marriage. My father didn't prevent her from continuing. I think what prevented her was her own depression. And as soon as I showed some signs of having a gift, she wanted to develop my gift rather than her own.

Later in life, my mother discovered that Ana, the

Spanish maid, wanted to paint. She encouraged Ana to become a naive artist, to the point that she even helped herself to some of my as yet unpainted canvases for Ana's use. I must say that her teaching was successful, since later, when Ana left us to go back to Spain, she was able to support herself with her colorful naive-style works.

My mother liked to develop anybody's gift but her own. More important, both my grandmothers were very forceful women, and I think sometimes after a strong generation there comes a less forceful one. But I'm strong, and so are my daughters, Paloma and Aurelia, so it depends on the individual.

My maternal grandmother was perhaps dominant, authoritarian. Some people are leaders, and others are followers. My mother was a happy girl, and she had the nature of an artist, or at least an applied artist. But I think losing the brother she adored in the war broke her spirit completely. That's when she became depressive.

Her brother was supposed to marry her best friend, who was from Argentina. Later her friend returned to Argentina. So the two people who were most important to my mother disappeared from her life. The other explanation might be that my mother paid so much attention to me. And economically, she didn't need to work.

LA: Your grandmother Gilot had to work because her husband died.

FG: Yes, but she worked even before his death because he had fragile health. He loved to make beautiful photographs and was a kind of poet, whereas she had a good grasp of business. In France, the roles of men and women are interchangeable. The attitude is that if you're the one who's more gifted in a particular area, why not do it?

Similarly, my maternal grandfather liked to do sculpture. So on both sides, the men were more artistic than the women, and the women handled the finances, at which they were excellent. Their husbands were delighted and encouraged their wives' business capabilities. Maybe I inherited a bit of that. Those roles of the breadwinner and all that are regarded as being for the birds in France. People do what they're good at.

LA: You're lucky. You got both.

FG: My mother decorated our house. She was also busy with sports. She was an excellent tennis player, a good mountain climber, a good shot with a rifle. And she was interested in the social scene, a bit like your Virginia grandmother. She was extremely well dressed and fashionable, especially for evening wear. She felt it was a woman's duty to uphold fashion in France. My father, an agronomist, was very capable at business, so her attitude was why should she do what he did better. Also, she was financially independent because she had a dowry in real estate from which she got income. So she did what she liked without having to worry about money.

My grandmothers' lives weren't destroyed, as my mother's was. My paternal grandmother was born in 1865, so she was five years old when the Franco-Prussian War began, but after that there was no war until 1914. There was no economic crisis in France, and as a young adult she was free to expand. She was wealthy before her marriage and came from a family that knew how to manage wealth.

My maternal grandmother was born in 1868, and it was the same thing: when she was a young adult, France was in complete economic expansion. It was the Third Republic. Although women didn't have the vote, the atmo-

Françoise's mother mountain climbing at age sixteen, Chamonix, France (1914).

sphere was one of equality between the sexes in terms of economic possibility. She was well educated and had a good mind.

My grandfather hated studies and was a kind of maverick artist who didn't believe in education in the least. He didn't even present himself for the exams, much less pass them. So no wonder his wife took over, even though their business belonged to his family.

Whereas for my mother, World War I began when she was sixteen and lasted until she was twenty. The brother she loved best was killed. She was in a kind of haze and allowed herself to marry my father, whom she didn't really love. I was born a year later, and she consecrated herself to me, but nothing ever really pleased her very much. She was in a kind of suspended animation. If there had been no war, she would have had a completely different destiny.

LA: Same as with you.

FG: Yes.

LA: My maternal great-grandmothers, who were the same generation as your grandmothers, both worked, but it was because they had to. In the case of my suffragist great-grandmother, her husband died when my grandfather was five. Then she married a man who blew off several fingers of one hand with a firecracker one July 4. He lit it and began to throw it, when the crowd closed in. Rather than letting it injure someone else, he closed his hand around it.

In the case of my chicken-breeding great-grandmother, her husband, a superintendent at an elevator company, fell down a shaft and was badly injured and had to stop working. So both my great-grandmothers helped support their families out of necessity.

FG: In Europe, because of all the wars people had learned that eventually bourgeois women might find themselves widows with young children. If they didn't have a profession that would maintain their social standing, they and their children might fall into poverty. That is a reason why education for women was so encouraged in France. Social status used to be a big thing there. If you fell from your class, that was terrible because your children would fall with you.

A proclamation of the Third Republic was that education should be free and equal for boys and girls. It was to be a question of the amount of gray matter in your head and nothing else. An intelligent girl was to have access to doing important things. That's why the future Madame Curie, a Polish woman, came to France, where she entered the École Supérieure de Physique et de Chimie with the result we all know, the discovery of radium. All the professions previously reserved for men opened up for women, too.

I think the determination to educate women came from the experience of all those wars. If all a woman knew how to do was to paint watercolors, she was doomed to paint watercolors on fans if her husband was killed. You earned no money for that or for needlework. It was considered important for women to have access to areas of the economy in which they could earn enough money to support themselves and their families if necessary.

Also, illness at that time was much more frequent than now. Your husband might have tuberculosis or cancer. That could happen very early.

LA: Both my grandfathers were ill. My paternal grandfather had pancreatic problems and had to have several operations. His wife, my Virginia grandmother, might have been so strong because she didn't have any choice. They owned real estate, but they were cash poor, and my father went to college on scholarships. My New York grandfather

was a bit of a hypochondriac and believed himself to be sick a lot. So the women in my family coped, while the men were often ill or dead.

FG: Both men and women at that time had strong survival skills because they had to, fortunately for their offspring. Many people had diseases that couldn't be treated in those days. They were alive, but they weren't well. There was no psychotherapy. Sometimes people became very sad and never got over it. Picasso's father looked like an Englishman, red-haired and blue-eyed, and his second daughter, Concepción, looked just like him. She died of diphtheria, and her father went into a deep depression for the rest of his life. That's when he gave his paints and brushes to Pablo, who was only fourteen.

Nowadays, we have no conception of what it could be like when people got depressed. No drugs, no therapy, nothing. On top of it all, it was supposed to be shameful, and you stayed home so nobody would see you. In Sicily, in each big house there was always one room for the insane person of the family.

LA: Like *Jane Eyre.*

FG: Yes, so the question often became, "Are you going to sit back and witness the fall of the house of Usher, or are you going to do something about it?" The women who had some character did something, pulled themselves together, and tried to maintain things.

So we are the descendants of winners, women who

won that struggle. The losers often didn't live to pass on their genes.

LA: I constantly think that if anything had happened to any one of my ancestors all the way back, I wouldn't be here today. My suffragist great-grandmother was reading the *Saturday Evening Post* and cut her finger on the edge of a page and died of septicemia. Fortunately for me, she'd long since given birth to my grandfather.

It must have been a whole different mind-set back then, when anything could kill you. These days so many people complain about all the horrible things that have happened to them, but we're the most fortunate people in the history of the world.

FG: Yes, with all the advances in surgery and medicine. That's why there are so many people on the face of the earth today. We are hostages to our successes. In most novels of the nineteenth century, you have a child dying, and that hardly happens anymore.

LA: When it does, it's a major tragedy. That's interesting that both you and Picasso had a depressive parent who turned the tools of the trade over to you.

But if we think about my great-grandmothers and your grandmothers being such accomplished women, the Edwardian period seems to have been a good time for women.

FG: It was the Belle Époque. Look how many positive images of women you find in the art of that period—the women are beautiful, elegant, and so on. It was the ascent of the bourgeoisie, the middle class. Many more people had access to education and art. And women were encouraged because they were new consumers, a new public for writers.

LA: And they weren't yet perceived as a threat.

FG: Right. It became harder afterward when there were more women demanding access to male preserves.

LA: Even the stereotypes, which were in some ways so stultifying, such as the angel of the hearth, were implying that women were repositories for the higher virtues.

FG: The angel of the hearth image is from early in the Victorian era, starting around 1840. I was talking rather about the Belle Époque, from 1871 to 1914, which I find more interesting because many women were out in the world making a mark and not just tending their homes. At that time, women were really at the top of the ladder. It was the generation of Colette, who was born in 1873. She was almost the first middle-class woman to become a writer.

Sarah Bernhardt, Lillie Langtry—the *demi-monde* and the *monde* began to overlap. There was very little distinction between the two. You could belong to both. The American writer Natalie Barney had as a mistress Madame Lantelme, who was a famous demimondaine. Lantelme's other lovers were famous men, grand dukes, and whatnot. Natalie Barney was also a friend of Colette's. Edith Wharton could have known them. Whether they liked one another or not is another question. The nuances between the gentry, the upper middle class, the aristocracy, the eccentrics, and the courtesans became blurred.

LA: Two things happened after that: First was World War I. It seems that when there's a war, masculine values are given primacy because the borders must be defended, so strength and violence come to the fore.

FG: I'm not so sure. Women go to work in the factories and become nurses. I think wars are the great social levelers. If you study the wars from the middle of the nineteenth century, you'll notice that with each one the social strata were flattened. Everything was destroyed, many people died, and afterward those who were left had to regroup, and they regrouped in less complex patterns than had existed before. That's why some people mourn the loss of their antebellum status.

War used to encourage masculine qualities, but men were also the ones who got killed, so it extinguished those qualities at the same time. Nowadays, if you have a war, everyone gets killed, so it's a different thing. War is the greatest hemorrhage of male energy that you can imagine. At the same time, women grab all the available positions.

In the United States, women were sent back to their kitchens afterward, but in Europe it was impossible because so many were widows. Widows of men killed in the war, if they didn't have jobs, had to be paid stipends by the government. So the government was in favor of having them work. This was true all over Europe.

When I was sixteen and said I wanted to be a painter, my father said I had to have a more serious job than that, like the law. "Don't forget that you may be a widow later on," he said. "There are wars all the time."

"But why study law?" I asked.

And he said, "If you're a widow, a knowledge of the law is an absolute must." He said studying law was the best thing a woman could do because if she had an abusive husband, she would also know what to do about it.

Since the seventeenth century in France, a number of authorities have been in favor of a thorough education for women. Fénelon, a very good writer, a cardinal or archbishop, tutor to a grandson of Louis XIV's, wrote a treatise saying women should have a broad education that included law because they were likely to become widows. Widowhood was like an obsession in Europe because of all the wars.

LA: The attitude that a woman had better be able to support herself since she may become a widow is an interesting one. It's the opposite here. When you visit the little country graveyards in Vermont or Tennessee, you see a man with three wives buried beside him, all of whom died quite young in childbirth. It was the men who were left widowers with small children.

The other thing that happened toward the end of the Belle Époque was that Freud and Havelock Ellis branded those intense female friendships during that period as lesbian. In the writings of Sarah Orne Jewett and others, the myth of Demeter and Persephone was very important, and many women had romantic friendships that sustained them as they worked in social services and for women's rights. Whether or not they were physical relationships is beside the point. But after the sexologists got finished with them, these friendships became suspect in the eyes of the public, and women became more wary of each other.

FG: But when did Henry James write *The Bostonians?* Eighteen eighty-six. The attack on Boston marriages was already under way then.

LA: I don't see that novel as an attack. James's sister, Alice, was living in a Boston marriage. He's satirical about the older woman, Olive. But he's also satirical about Basil, the man who takes the younger woman, Verena, away from her.

The last sentence, when Verena is fleeing the lecture platform in tears, knowing she will leave Olive to marry Basil, is "It is to be feared that with the union, so far from brilliant, into which she was about to enter, these were not the last she was destined to shed."

I think James meant the story as a tragedy. Could Olive ever really hope to overcome Verena's biology and conditioning?

Nevertheless, until World War I and Freud, the Belle Époque was a positive one for women, and my great-grandmothers and your grandmothers flourished. Women in America finally got the vote in 1920 after seventy years of effort over three generations. But afterward, your mother and my Rochester grandmother didn't flourish. Why not?

FG: In addition to World War I, there was the Depression, don't forget—although it wasn't felt as strongly in Europe as here, and it was felt later. The upheavals there were mostly political, with Hitler in Germany and Mussolini in Italy.

It's typical of the American way of life that those women got organized and worked tirelessly through three generations to achieve the vote, all through women's forming groups and volunteering their time and effort. In France, women are often so individualistic that they find it silly to work with one another.

LA: In my generation, women volunteers in every region of the country started rape crisis centers, battered-women shelters. I worked for several years at Planned Parenthood in Vermont as a birth control and abortion counselor. I was also on the board there and ran informational programs at schools. A large group of women prominent in that area formed the first abortion clinic. Many of us went to Washington for the pro-choice demonstrations and marches.

I'm not involved in any of that at the moment, because I'm traveling too much, but I feel guilty. Whenever I'm between novels, I start wanting to go to midwifery school in Kentucky so I can ride a mule and deliver babies in the backwoods. For better or for worse, it's built into the culture.

You said Frenchwomen got the vote immediately after World War II because they had proved themselves in the Resistance?

FG: Between World War I and II, it had been debated more than once. The Chamber of Deputies passed a law giving women the vote, but the Senate repealed it each time.

But after World War II, there was very little debate because so many women had participated in the Resistance or were coming back from the concentration camps. People said, "Well, if they have fought, suffered, and died just like men, they can vote just like men."

LA: It was the same with the Cherokees in the region in which I grew up. Some women fought alongside the men, so they were given equal rights and respect. Every person belonged to one of the seven clans. Each clan had a clan mother, and they picked the chief, who was a man. The head clan mother was called the Beloved Woman.

When a couple married, they moved into the woman's home. In case of divorce, which either could initiate, the man had to return to his mother's household, while the woman stayed in her home with their children.

The tribe never went to war unless the council of women okayed it. The rationale was that since their sons were the warriors, the mothers had the right to approve of putting their sons at risk.

The Cherokee version of the expulsion from Eden—rather than featuring an evil woman who lures an innocent man with an apple supplied by a snake—involves young men who are expelled from paradise because they show disrespect to their grandmother.

When the European settlers and the Cherokees had their first meeting, the Cherokees looked at all the white men and asked, "But where are your women?" They couldn't fathom holding a high-level meeting with no women present. I guess it's been downhill ever since.

Many people in my region have Cherokee ancestry. When the U.S. government rounded the Cherokees up in 1838 and marched them to Oklahoma on the Trail of Tears, some escaped and hid out in the mountains and intermarried with European settlers. Others already married to Europeans were allowed to stay. Aspects of the Cherokee worldview permeate that region to this day, including their respect for strong women.

Learning a bit about this legacy has helped me understand how my grandmother could be such a force of nature. She ran the family, and she ran the town. My grandfather deferred to her, and so did my father. He was protective of my mother and encouraged his daughters to regard ourselves as at least the equals of men.

Generalizing from all the violence he had to mop up after in the emergency room, he used to maintain that men were emotionally handicapped and that women were their superiors. He taught my sister and me to shoot guns and drive his Jeep in the hills and ride horses, just as he did my brothers. He encouraged us to go to college and pick professions, just as he did the boys.

FG: Equality of deeds brings equality of rights. As long as a woman is being protected and must stay inside the home, she is regarded as a second-class person who isn't entirely adult.

LA: Yes. Firewomen, policewomen—it's not irrelevant that women are now doing those jobs. It's interesting that the women of the Gauls also fought alongside their men, and now Frenchwomen get a lot of respect compared with women elsewhere. Maybe it's a holdover from the distant past, as well as a result of their working for the Resistance. But of course Israeli women don't get that much respect, and they fight in the army alongside the men.

FG: In religions where monotheism is strict, with devotion being directed toward a male god without so much as female saints, there is no status for women. That's what you find in Judaism and Islam. Transcendence concerns only men. Women are regarded as supernumerary, soulless creatures just good for making children, cooking dinner, and providing pleasure.

It's interesting that the personalities of some of the women who have been important to you—your mother, your Virginia grandmother, your suffragist great-grandmother—are so different. They don't duplicate each other in the least. Each imparted different qualities. It's like how all the tributaries make a large river.

LA: Yes, it's like nutrients for a plant. One gives magnesium, one calcium, and so on. If I think about those women, I can probably find things to criticize, but I can also see how each provided me with a crucial role model.

Every generation stands on the shoulders of the generations that precede it. That's why I get annoyed when I hear young women repudiating feminism, even as they enjoy the rights we've managed to acquire. But when you're an attractive young thing, men tend to cater to you. I guess it takes reaching early old age to see the situation more clearly.

5. THE LITTLE BLACK DRESS

LA: When I arrived at Wellesley College in 1962, I felt completely out of place, coming as I did from a small town in Tennessee to this Seven Sisters college near Boston. Wellesley was founded in 1870 with the goal of giving young women an education equivalent to the one young men were receiving at Harvard, Princeton, and Yale. "The Wellesley Girl" was supposed to be brainy and attractive and socially poised.

When I walked down the sidewalks on campus, I automatically smiled at passersby whom I didn't know and said hello, as we did back home. But they said nothing and gave me glances that indicated they thought I was insane.

I had placed second in my high school class, but many there were valedictorians. I had been a swimming star back home, so I joined the swim team. But at the first practice, by the time I made it to the end of the pool, everyone else had already done a flip turn and returned to the opposite end. Some had been in the Junior Olympics.

In class, I was getting Ds and Fs. I'd never even written an essay before. For our senior English project in high school, we were supposed to assemble a model to illustrate a short story we'd read. I chose "The Lagoon" by Joseph Conrad. I glued a mirror on a piece of plywood and rubbed brown shoe polish all over it. Then I made a bank of moss. I glued together toothpicks to make a hut, which I roofed with straw. I made a toothpick dock and a canoe of birch bark, and that was my senior thesis.

FG: I've never heard of such a thing! It's marvelous!

LA: On an English test in high school, the teacher asked for a synonym for "perdition." I wrote "damnation," and she counted it wrong because it wasn't "hell." I went to the library and found a dictionary that listed "damnation" as a synonym for "perdition" and carried it to her.

She said, "That's just one dictionary. I bet they're not all like that." And she still counted my answer half-wrong.

So this was the kind of preparation I'd had for Wellesley. I worked all the time there because I wanted to do well, until I ended up in the infirmary for a month with mononucleosis.

My friends fixed me up with dates with young men at the Ivy League colleges. You'd get on a bus, and when you got off, this guy you'd never seen before would be waiting for you. If you liked each other, you had a good time. But if you didn't, it was a nightmare because you were stuck spending a weekend with a stranger you didn't like who didn't like you.

Many Wellesley students were genuine debutantes— the New York and Philadelphia kind, not the Tennessee kind. What it meant to dress well in their terms was something I'd never even contemplated. But I soon discovered the Little Black Dress! Everyone owned one, or several. And this was a great relief to me because I now knew at least one thing: what I was supposed to wear. It was a uniform. You took one when you went away to weekends at men's colleges. Your Little Black Dress and heels and pearls, and that was it. I had finally discovered how to fit in.

FG: The second year did you do better, academically speaking?

LA: I seemed to have the ability to pick up what was expected of me. I was so much of an outsider that I could see very clearly what was inside. The way to write a good paper was to take your professor's opinions and write them up with footnotes, and then you got an A. I was very cynical about it. I ended up doing well. Once I got into English literature, I developed a passion for my work, and everything clicked.

FG: You were unprepared for the standards there, but within a year you were able to function. That's the survival instinct at work. What years did you spend at Wellesley?

LA: Nineteen sixty-two to 1966. Just at the beginning of the countercultural revolution in America. So I guess the Little Black Dress was a holdover from the 1950s. In those days, Wellesley itself was a holdover from the 1950s. We were photographed in our underwear, and those with poor posture had to attend remedial classes. We also took speech tests, and those with nonstandard accents were retrained. I just barely passed, thanks to my mother, who had attempted to moderate my brothers' and my east Tennessee drawls throughout our childhoods.

We were required to take a course freshman year called Fundamentals of Movement, in which we learned how to pick up an overnight bag while wearing spike heels, how to sink into a couch while balancing a cocktail glass, how to get into a sports car without flashing too much thigh. I'd never even ridden in a sports car before.

FG: What did you wear day-to-day at Wellesley?

LA: It was very casual. Wheat-colored jeans and turtlenecks in your room or at the library. Wool skirts and sweaters and flats to class and to dinner. Unless you woke up late. I remember several times dashing to class with a raincoat over my nightgown.

FG: Stockings or panty hose?

LA: It was still stockings then, with a girdle.

FG: When I was a child in the 1930s, women wore those famous Scandale girdles, which gave a very flat look to the profile. An American writer just after the war called it the style of the "one-buttocked woman." But in my generation, we didn't want just one buttock. During World War II, there were no stockings, so we painted our legs with foundation cream and wore small white briefs.

After the war, we wore just little *porte-jarretelles,* garter belts to hold up the stockings. Men liked these very much; it was a part of the myth! When panty hose came in, they didn't like it at all. But all the women were happy because panty hose were convenient, easy to wear, and less replete with sexual connotations.

When I first came to the United States in 1961, I saw that most women still wore girdles, and I couldn't believe it. There was even a type of girdle with legs that came all the way from the knees up to the waist. The women couldn't breathe. With the built-in garters, there was no space between the tops of the stockings and the legs of the girdle. That, I thought, was antierotic to the extreme. In France, the idea was that especially if the stocking were dark, you had that area of lighter flesh between the stocking and the panty.

LA: No, girdles are definitely not erotic. In fact, they're almost impossible to circumvent.

FG: Maybe that's why there are more rapes nowadays.

LA: Yes, when women wore girdles, men bounced right back out again, like on a trampoline.

FG: But back to the Little Black Dress. *La petite robe noire*—the actual term originated with Chanel. In France, the concept comes from a rather pragmatic notion: people used to say that you always needed a Little Black Dress because you would be in mourning many times in your life.

LA: I don't think it has that connotation here at all. Do people in France these days recognize its origins in mourning?

FG: Certainly not, because nowadays people don't observe such long mourning periods, and we don't have such all-engrossing wars. Now you do it for six months for a close relative like your parents, your spouse, your brothers or sisters. Not to do so is considered disrespectful. But when I was a child, it was still really serious. For six months, black and white. For another six months, black, white, gray, and purple.

Sometimes in France a widow adopted a wardrobe that was basically black, white, gray, and purple permanently.

My maternal grandmother stayed in perpetual mourning for her beloved son who died in World War I, wearing only black and white forever after. My paternal grandmother's husband died in 1911, and I never saw her in anything other than black or white, until she died in 1943. She had an admirer who wanted to marry her, but her wardrobe was her way of saying no. If a widow meant not to marry again, she would never come out of mourning. A man who liked her would know "ce n'est pas la peine d'essayer." If a widow decided to marry again, she had to adopt colorful clothes.

My paternal grandmother's eldest daughter, Jeanne, was widowed during World War I, and she wore only black, white, gray, and purple from 1916 until her death in 1980. I was very fond of her and she liked me a lot, so she would come to all my exhibitions in Paris. On such official occasions, she would be entirely in black, a black hat, a black coat, black purse, shoes, and stockings. She would stop in front of various paintings and stand there for a long time, and I would wonder if she were ever going to move on, or was she going to stand there in black forevermore. It wasn't very nice of me, but I was annoyed. It made my openings sad to have her practicing her widowhood right there in front of my paintings. Having been a widow since 1916, she could at least have worn a colorful scarf, it seemed to me. Of course, I never said a word to her about it because she had decided to be a professional widow.

LA: Do people observe mourning all over Europe?

FG: I bet in Italy and Spain and even in Germany it's just the same. I don't know about England. They love tweed so much, and tweeds aren't black.

Sometimes customs are more prevalent among the

working classes than in the bourgeoisie. By and large, in the provinces mourning is still observed. And more so the farther south you go. Not to do so shows you don't care. Again, it's a silent form of speech.

But if you are out of work, you may not have the resources to change wardrobes. It's a part of old traditions that are disappearing fast. In ten years, it may be finished completely, but fifty years ago it was very important. It's like the disappearance of dialects and accents because of television. I think television is making things more uniform. People want to be like everyone else. Also, it's become more important now to have a second car than a second wardrobe for mourning.

LA: I guess the European immigrants coming to the United States just dropped a lot of the old proprieties.

FG: I think so. Maybe they even came here because they wanted to drop all that. Also, many times when they arrived, they were extremely poor. And by the time they became affluent, they'd forgotten the old ways.

LA: So the Little Black Dress endures, but the original meaning has been lost.

FG: When I first came to the United States in the early 1960s, the concept of the Little Black Dress didn't seem to be at all prevalent. Whenever I went to dinner somewhere, I was surprised to see the women wearing gowns all the way to the floor. Whereas in France, unless it was really a very important celebration, women didn't attend a dinner party dressed in gowns. They usually preferred a simple Little Black Dress.

Some women preferred dark brown as a basic solid color. Others preferred navy blue. But in many families, through the loss of relatives, so many months or years were spent in mourning that it was practical to have basic clothes in black. When you were not in mourning, you added cheerful colors, and when you were in mourning, you added white, and that was it.

In Brittany, for example, there are some islands, like the Île de Sein and the Île d'Ouessant, where women used to wear black all their lives. Their husbands, fathers, and sons being fishermen and the ocean, the currents, the tides in those areas being so dangerous, they had lost or were going to lose a number of male relatives, so they adopted the tradition of black local costumes.

LA: But you couldn't wear a sleeveless, low-cut black dress and be in mourning, could you?

FG: Well, sure. A short jacket can be added, or a cardigan. The cut has nothing to do with mourning; it's the color. Also, the Little Black Dress must be such that you can wear it at the office if you're a workingwoman. And by changing the accessories, you can use it as a dinner dress as well.

LA: I remember going to a dinner party in New York when I bought my apartment here in 1991, and all the men were in dark suits and ties, and all the women were in Little Black Dresses. There was no adornment anywhere, and it was indeed like going to a wake or a Quaker meeting. But you're saying that the idea in France is to buy a few pieces of basic clothing and then dress them up with colorful accessories?

FG: Yes. In France, most women have a few good items that they will wear for many years, embellishing them with different accessories. For example, you can match royal blue or silver shoes with a black dress. The stockings can be of a different texture. The piece may be inconspicuous by itself, but the scarf, the jewelry, a little bolero, or a very short jacket will make it intriguing.

It must be a showcase for the body, so it follows that the body has to look good. That's an incentive to practice some sports. Even if a Frenchwoman loves sweets and cookies, she is not going to eat them, because she wants to look seductive.

LA: You once said that in France, women conceal their defects, reveal their assets, and offer nothing. Whereas American women tend either to conceal their bodies or to offer them.

FG: Yes, that's why I don't consider paying attention to appearance a superficial thing; it's a way for a woman to express herself. In Europe, we aren't concerned so much with fashion as with the concept of the adornment of the body as an art form.

If you have not looked closely at yourself, you certainly do not realize what the good points are in your face and figure. By and large, European women understand what suits them, and if the fashion is bad for them one year, they are not going to buy anything that year. For example, if your legs aren't perfect, you aren't going to wear a mini-skirt. You'll instead buy a pair of long velvet pants. But to compensate for your bad points, you have to know what they are.

LA: One of the ways you know what yours are is because

your mother and grandmothers draped colors on you when you were just five years old, and discussed which ones looked best.

FG: Yes, I was consulted, and if I didn't like a color or a particular style, they would not select it, since I was likely to throw a tantrum otherwise!

This critiquing also happened at school. I was among the smallest because I was younger than most in my class, and I was thin, so I didn't stand out like a sore thumb and was not bullied. The girls who suffered were the ones who were fat. They were criticized openly, because in France even children are unrelenting against fat. It's funny that a nation that likes food so much hates fat so much. The good food is for men, not for women.

So in my class at school, there was a girl who was called Béatrice or Gaétane, some such beautiful name. She was quite plump, and she tried to hide it by bending over. So we were all after her: "What do you eat, why are you like this, stand up, be erect." It was really awful. We were quite cruel. But we acted with a missionary zeal.

And I know that in this country it's very politically incorrect. But the result is that there are many more obese people in the United States than in Europe. In Europe, people criticize each other more freely, and it's done very early in life, so maybe it doesn't hurt that much.

LA: I think it's demoralizing to have your appearance criticized no matter at what age or by whom. Did that ever happen to you?

FG: I learned from a friend that I needed one more inch between my knees and my ankles. She said, "What a pity, because otherwise your figure would be perfect." So that was a defect I had not seen myself, and I almost cried because I realized I was not perfect in her eyes. I had a tendency not to be as truthful with her because I wanted to increase her self-confidence. So, although she had fairly ample hips and thighs, I thought they suited her well.

She used to complain, "Oh, my thighs are like hams, isn't it terrible?"

And I would answer that they were just right. Sometimes, in friendship, the need to be truthful is not essential.

When I met her, she was thirteen, but she looked eighteen or nineteen because, being from Languedoc, she was already a fully developed woman. She had breasts, and she had a figure that was quite shapely and feminine. With her classical look, her face and figure were in harmony. The proportion of each part to the whole was perfect. She had very small hands and feet. Being slightly plump suited her. She was too lazy to exercise. Whenever she came out of her lethargy, she could be a fantastic skier, but she would come into action only once in a while, and otherwise she would relax and say, "It's too cold (or too warm) to do anything."

But she was obsessed with the dictates of fashion. Maybe that's a difference between being born in Paris and in the provinces, because in the provinces reading *Vogue* and the other fashion magazines is very important. Whereas in Paris, you have direct access to the designer clothes and to the department stores, and you watch everybody else. You are already aware of how to determine your own style. I don't remember buying *Vogue,* except very seldom.

LA: *Vogue* promotes one ideal, and right now it's incredibly tall and anorexic. It makes me wonder if the photographers are misogynists who are disgusted by really feminine bodies like your friend's, with hips and thighs and breasts.

FG: The *Vogue* ideal was exactly like that back then, too. I always felt it was artificial, and it didn't impress me. I was already well aware, on account of my family, of what it took to be well dressed. Revealing a bit of who you are without offering yourself. Hiding small defects, but without exaggeration.

I remember that my friend, who had the most perfect breasts one can imagine, was in the habit of fitting the straps of her brassiere so tightly that she would hurt the flesh of her shoulders. For some absurd reason, she wanted her breasts to be almost at shoulder level. And I remarked, "It's not necessary, why do that?"

LA: But the majority of Frenchwomen appear to be short and slender, which makes me suspect that it's partly genetic.

FG: Ah, but we're small because we don't eat at home the type of food served in the restaurants. Many people earn a bit less money than in the United States for similar jobs, and they spend their money in a different way—on good clothes or a nice apartment. In France, you would not mind having a silly little car in order to have a more beautiful apartment.

It's sometimes in the working-class districts of Paris that you find the most appetizing food because people there spend more money on food than in the areas that are well-to-do. Conversely, people who live near Avenue Victor Hugo, where beautiful fashion shops are in abundance, will spend more money on their wardrobes.

In the early 1960s, during my divorce from Luc Simon,

{ 155 }

I had a friend who had been recently widowed who was also experiencing difficult times. So we would call each other and ask, "How are you feeling?"

"Not too good."

"Not too good? How bad?"

"Maybe bad enough for a scarf at Hermès."

So we'd go buy scarves for each other and come home feeling rather pleased, with our moods improved.

If we felt really terrible, one of us might say, "Well, let's go to Cardin and see what they have."

It could be an occasion for a hat, or for some costume jewelry, or for a dress. The superficial part of yourself takes over, and you feed your mutual narcissism by saying, "Oh, this color suits you very well." You feel better, at least for a time.

LA: Shopping therapy. When one of my relationships ended, I went to the mall a lot and bought clothes. Usually I was alone, but it did cheer me up.

FG: But it's three times as effective with a friend. It becomes a kind of ceremony. Then we'd go have tea somewhere and compliment each other on our purchases.

LA: In France, so many people smoke, and when you stop smoking, you gain, on the average, ten pounds, because your metabolism slows down. One of your French friends told me that when his sister got to be about thirteen, she put on weight, as pubescent girls often do, and that his mother insisted she start smoking to try to get the weight off.

FG: That doesn't astonish me. My father didn't smoke at all, and my mother smoked very little. But when I was about thirteen, I was told I could smoke as much as I wanted, because they thought that if they forbade me to smoke, I would smoke all my life. So of course I was very pleased, and from age thirteen to eighteen I was smoking two packs a day. In fact, I wasn't inhaling, so it was mostly for show. Finally, being very proud of the fact that I swam well and fast, and seeing that it wasn't so good for my breathing, I decided to stop.

Many times in Europe, parents and children are more indirect in the way they relate to one another. When they want something, they pursue it in a more oblique manner. They say, "You can smoke all you want," thinking that after the excess satiety will follow.

LA: I used to forbid my daughter to chew gum, partly because I hated chewing gum but also because I thought then she'd sneak around chewing gum instead of shooting heroin or something. So maybe things aren't all that different in the United States. Or at least not among southerners, who are known for rarely saying what they really mean.

My parents smoked after dinner every evening when I was growing up. They stopped when the surgeon general's report linking smoking to cancer came out, and forever afterward they denied that they had ever smoked, which sometimes made me question my sanity.

When I was a teenager, I discovered a pack of cigarettes in my brother's closet. I smoked one every now and then, huddled in the closet. I'm sure my mother must have smelled the smoke, but she never said a word. Nor did my brother ever comment on his missing cigarettes. I felt very risqué. Sometimes as my friends and I cruised around town in a friend's Thunderbird, we smoked cigarettes stolen from someone's mother. But once I went to Wellesley, where students were allowed to smoke as much as they wanted, it seemed much less appealing. Those legal cigarettes never tasted as good as the stolen and forbidden ones!

The other day you said that French clothes are either close fitting or flowing and that American clothes are usually somewhat boxy?

FG: What used to be considered basic in France was a tailor, usually a man, expert at making riding habits. Clothing cut close to the body, fitting well yet allowing movement, is the basic goal of the French or Italian tailor, and those tailors captured a part of the designer's field.

For example, when I was growing up, Lucien Lelong, a man's tailor who even made military uniforms for officers, went into fashion for women. Pierre Cardin started out there. Cardin came from Italy, where he had learned the same type of cut. There is little difference between making a coat or a jacket for a man or a woman in France or Italy, except that women have breasts. Yves Saint Laurent represents that type of cut.

The other face of fashion is what I call the flowing style, which came mostly from the great women designers like Madeleine Vionnet, Madame Lanvin. Inspired by Isadora Duncan, they wanted to liberate the body from the corset and other artificial hindrances.

The story of fashion is a bit the history of women's gaining freedom from the constrictions in their clothing made mostly to appeal to men's sensuality, like the whalebone corset, which so compressed the lower part of the lung that many women would faint. They could hardly breathe.

The best-known woman designer, Madeleine Vionnet, whom I met when I was five years old, was a friend

Dress worn by Françoise at age five, when she met Madeleine Vionnet for the first time (1926).

of my grandmother's. One of Madame Vionnet's friends, Madame Michonnet, was also a friend of my grandmother's. Her husband, Monsieur Michonnet, along with Monsieur Lesage, created all the lace and embroideries for Madeleine Vionnet.

But his wife resolutely refused to wear that type of fashion, so she still had a corset and was always short of breath. I nicknamed her "the Mountain" because, although the lower part of her body was like everybody else's, then it went up vertically like a cliff to form a horizontal shelf. Her corset brought her abundant breasts nearly to her neck. She would lift me up from the ground and place me on top of that platform of breasts in order to kiss me. It gave me vertigo. I thought Madame "la Montagne" must be somebody special because she seemed to be breathing up and down like a bellows, not sideways like everybody else. I thought she must have special lungs.

But you can see posters of paintings from the turn of the century in which all the workingwomen are depicted just as tightly corseted. So I don't know how they managed.

LA: The corset is one of the ways in which women's bodies were contorted into unnatural shapes in order to appeal to men sexually, particularly in terms of making women seem feeble.

FG: Yes, transforming the Other into a sex object, as opposed to a sex subject. But the Chinese custom of foot binding was much worse. Women of the upper classes were subjected to it, and they became incapable of walking on their own and thus couldn't leave a bad situation on foot!

It supposedly had an erotic appeal similar to shoe fetishism in Europe. Extremely pointed shoes may be considered phallic. In vulgar French, *prendre son pied*, to take one's foot, means to masturbate. The Chinese transformed the female foot itself into a fetish and at the same time prevented the women from walking, killing two birds with one stone.

LA: That making women more feeble could be erotically stimulating is an odd thought.

FG: I don't know if making women weaker was the point so much as the fetishism of the foot.

LA: So it's a question of fashions that changed the perceived shape of the female body, and also of the things that were done to a woman's body to change it in fact. Those poor little crippled feet of Chinese women were called lotuses, and men would insert their penises into the holes formed by the broken feet. And of course genital mutilation in Africa.

FG: In comparison to foot binding and genital mutilation, the artificiality in Europe didn't really touch the body itself, only attempting to reveal it as different from what it really is.

LA: But what about liposuction and face-lifts?

FG: Wait a minute, don't confuse the issues. Women do that to themselves. We have to make a distinction between transformations imagined by men and applied to women, with their consent or not, in the name of fashion or custom or caste, and things that women do to themselves, like cosmetic surgery, to satisfy their own vanity.

LA: But the mothers did the foot binding and genital mutilation.

FG: Yes, but the mothers did it so that their daughters would be like everybody else and not be rejected. When a Muslim mother tells her daughter aged thirteen to wear a veil, it just means that she has internalized the customs. Of course in India, it's so dusty that wearing a veil makes sense. So sometimes there are origins to customs that are completely in keeping with the climate or other life conditions.

LA: But along with the veil go the robes that conceal the shape of the body.

FG: In hot climates, though, you are attacked by the elements when you go out—sandstorms and all that. So the robes originated as protection against the elements, but then they became artificial, first a necessity, then a custom, then a religious obligation. When people first began not eating pork, for example, it was because of trichinosis. So at first it was hygienic, but then it became religious. So many prohibitions begin for plausible reasons, but then they become sacralized in ways that are detrimental to specific groups.

But something like foot binding was entirely artificial from its inception. It's a fetishism of the foot parallel to sewing closed the vulva. These are ways of maiming the individual that never served a plausible function. You can't put everything in the same bag.

LA: But both fashion and those kinds of maiming practices have in common an inability to accept the female body as it is.

FG: Many times the male body is also altered. The ancient Egyptians put bandages around the head of a male baby to give him a conical cranium because they thought this would develop the intellectual faculties. Or what about the tattoos and scarification of some African tribes, which are done primarily to males? Such practices can be seen as a mark of recognition for belonging to a certain tribe, like circumcision for the Jews and the Arabs.

Of course when such alterations are done to girls, it is usually to make them into sex objects. But something like circumcision must leave a wound, or at least a trace, on the male psyche. Their sexual behavior may be different from those who have not been circumcised.

LA: It's the threat of castration that Freud talks about so much.

FG: Right. If the child is very young, it can mark the psyche forever. The Lord says, "It shall be a sign of alliance between me and you." But that alliance may result in psychological trauma. With Muslims, it's done when the boy is about seven, and some of them even die. It's done to make them become part of a certain theological order, to induce an irreversible identification.

LA: It's almost like branding a steer.

FG: Each culture tries to impose a sense of membership on its young people, both boys and girls, and tries to impart its values through various rituals. One form alters some parts of their very bodies.

Another form involves adding appendages, to change the appearance of the body without changing the body itself. Men in the seventeenth century, for example, wore those ridiculous powdered wigs, even if they had hair underneath. And in the Middle Ages, men wore *souliers à la poulaine* (crakows with upturned and pointed toes). Such shoes were worn even to ride a horse, which is absurd.

The third form has to do with customs that were initiated for some practical or hygienic reason and then became religious obligations.

In May 1956, just after the independence of Tunisia, when women were no longer obliged to wear veils (though most of them still did), I went to a beach not far from Carthage. I wore a bikini, as I usually did in France, and I could sense that even though I came with my husband, Luc Simon, some Muslim friends with us seemed rather shocked. I thought, "What's the matter with them? Isn't this what all women wear on the beach?"

Then I saw some Muslim women entering the sea in their robes and veils. They rolled up their robes as they went in, to keep them dry. Little by little you could see their legs, their thighs, their buttocks, their backs, et cetera. You saw all their anatomy, whereas my bikini, as small as it was, was hiding the essentials. They stood there in the sea for a long time, not moving, just talking to each other with their robes in bundles on top of their heads. (The Mediterranean is quite calm, with no surf to speak of.)

As they turned to come back in, they progressively unrolled their garments, but as they didn't want them to touch the water, there was always a moment during which you could see first their breasts, then their navels, their tummies, their pubic areas, their thighs.

I said to my Muslim friends, "Isn't that shocking? I've seen their entire anatomy."

And they answered, "Yes, but thanks to the veils on the faces, you don't know who they are."

In the last two decades of the nineteenth century, male designers dreamed up an artifice called *tournure*, or *faux cul* in the vernacular, which was a padding worn beneath the back of the dress to achieve the kind of abstract shapes we find in Georges Seurat's paintings. Many men have a fetishism for the buttocks, and the *faux cul* was invented to add to the buttocks. A woman very slim in front, thanks to the padding in back, appeared to have protruding buttocks. That padding was called *avantages*, advantages, because it was thought to make a woman's shape more advantageous.

During the eighteenth century, it was *les paniers*, the baskets, on the sides of dresses, additions that have nothing to do with female anatomy. In the Middle Ages, women wore the hennin, the long conical headgear with a veil. All those shapes were accentuating some aspect of the body in an artificial way, the more artificial, the better.

But then came Isadora Duncan, Ruth St. Denis, Martha Graham, several generations of women dancers who showed what was possible when the female body was freed from its constraints. Simultaneously came the women designers. The first generation was *les sœurs* Callot and Madeleine Vionnet, Madame Lanvin soon thereafter, and then Chanel. Schiaparelli, Nina Ricci. Madame Grès began at the outset of World War II.

Madeleine Vionnet started to cut fabric on the bias so that it would swirl and flow, escaping from the stern laws of gravity, so to speak. And then Madame Grès draped silk and jersey fabric into folds, making pleats, as in a Grecian tunic. It was tight-fitting but always on the bias, so it followed the movements of the woman who was wearing it.

The taste for flowing fabric originated from the influence of Isadora Duncan. She came to France early in her life and was very much admired. She danced almost stark naked wearing light, flowing tunics—and no corset, of course. She insisted that women needed to exercise to build firm, well-shaped bodies so as not to need brassieres or girdles. Her example was very inspiring to many women. For example, my grandmother regarded Isadora Duncan as a great artist, a woman hero, for maintaining that a woman's body shouldn't be made into something artificial and weak.

In the 1930s, when I was a child, many women adored sports. They were hiking, mountain climbing, skiing, playing tennis and golf, shooting. My mother, for example, was almost a tennis champion. So these women had athletic bodies. They were not the women of the first decade of the twentieth century at all, females who had those tiny waists, were plump in some places and thin in others.

Sports in my mother's youth was a new conquest for women. At the beginning of the century, trying to play tennis or ski in a long skirt or riding a horse sidesaddle was a decorative activity rather than a sport. After World War I, women started to ride astride, with riding britches like men, and to wear shorts to play tennis.

In the early twentieth century, the Callot sisters began to simplify fashion, and women designers like Chanel simplified further. On holidays, Chanel had gone to England with friends and had started wearing men's sports sweaters. Her revolution was to find seamstresses who could work with very nice hand- or machine-woven jersey in wool or silk.

So the great revolution came from women designers and from dancers such as Isadora Duncan. The male designers always tried to get away from nature rather than to help natural grace and ease.

My definitely modern grandmother was wearing those

flowing things (some expensive ones from Madame Vionnet and everyday ones made at home), with long scarves
(like the one that killed Isadora Duncan) twisted around
her neck and falling almost to the ground on both sides.

LA: When you were talking about male designers doing
a tailored look, you said that the jackets they made for
women were not so different from what they made for
men, apart from allowing for the breasts. This is another
example of the ways in which the French and the Italians
seem more androgynous than people in northern Europe
and America.

FG: Yes, Anglo-Saxon men are often taller and more mus-
cular. Italian and French men are more nervous and lean.
In the United States, the armholes around the shoulders
in a man's jacket are usually extremely broad.

My second husband, Jonas Salk, who was born in New
York but was from an immigrant family from Lithuania,
had a European body type. Soon after I met him, I told
him that those nice Brooks Brothers clothes he wore did
not suit him because they were much too big around the
shoulders and upper arms. As soon as I could persuade him
to buy clothes in France and Italy, they suited him perfectly, even ready-made.

On women, the cut is tight-fitting while still allowing movement. But that doesn't mean that the finished
product looks masculine. It can be quite well adapted to
a woman's body. By the time of my childhood, women's
bodies had been liberated from the corset and all that.
Women were doing sports and had well-exercised bodies that, apart from the breasts, were similar to those of
eighteen-year-old males.

When I was growing up, I noticed that in department stores I could buy the same shirt that was being sold in the girls' section in the boys' section for a third of the price. The only difference was that it buttoned on the opposite side. When I was skiing in the Alps early in the spring and it was really warm, I'd wear one unbuttoned to my navel with no brassiere. My boyfriend would ask why I didn't button it, because I might catch cold, or because if I fell, snow might get inside it. And I'd reply that I couldn't button it, because the buttons were on the wrong side!

You've said, very rightly, that in France people are a bit more androgynous. Men can be not effeminate but more feminine. When my father recited poetry, which he did well, he could be very moved and cry over a beautiful verse. He was very masculine, but he did not prevent himself from crying.

In France, men and women are always together. They enjoy each other's company at work and at home. Most of the time, relationships are not sexual. But there is much more interaction, the war of the sexes is not so intense. It exists, but it's not so destructive.

LA: Did you agree with what it said in that book *French or Foe?* about the French getting dressed up whenever they go out of the house because they never know when they might meet "the one"?

FG: Yes, that book is fun and accurate. I remember that my mother did not mind wearing the same outfits outside as well as inside the house, but my father said nobody could go out of our home without being properly attired because it reflected on the good name of the whole extended family.

Years later in Paris, as a would-be artist, I sometimes wore a Brittany fisherman's outfit with a blue shrimp-catching net on my hair. If he saw me coming, my father would cross to the other side of the street so as not to say hello to me. He was really offended by my eccentricities. But conversely, he would be generous if I wanted to get fashionable and expensive outfits at Lucien Lelong, especially in white, his favorite color (for me). When I wore these, he would cross the street to greet me!

Elegance is not considered frivolous in France. Men also participate in the belief that fashion lends dignity and status, that it is a way to represent France. We create fashion, perfumes, and other luxury products. When exported, they bring to France more than the sale of cars. Even if exporting cars could bring good profits, it costs a lot of money to make them, whereas it doesn't cost that much to produce fashion items. It's a very important source of income for the country.

LA: So Frenchwomen are like a walking advertisement for the French economy?

FG: Right. When I started to go to the United States in 1961, I dressed mostly at Pierre Cardin, where the number one saleswoman, called "la Première," happened to be the same one I had known as first saleswoman at Lucien Lelong years before. She always kept dresses from the collection for me. I would get them for half price, to be representing France when traveling in the United States.

LA: Just to interject some contrast, during my childhood I was wearing hand-me-downs from my older brother. I had two pairs of shoes, Keds sneakers and sturdy oxfords. But

Lisa biking barefoot at age eight (1952).

I went barefoot the entire summer, except when I went downtown or to church. In the summer, I wore shorts and a T-shirt, and in cooler weather, jeans and a T-shirt or flannel shirt. At school, I wore cotton dresses because I was forced to. But I wanted to wear jeans as my brothers did.

When I became a teen, I bought wool skirts and sweater sets and shirtwaist dresses for school, but my goal was to not stand out in any way and to look exactly like every other girl in my school.

FG: Yes, but in France we make a big difference between everyday clothes and the clothes you wear during the weekend if you go somewhere. Everyday clothes can be old and utilitarian, just as in the United States. When children go to school, what is important is to dress them in a way that is not impeding their movements or making them look different from their classmates. Paloma wore a number of things that Claude had worn before her to go to school. So everyday clothes that were of good quality to begin with might be threadbare toward the end. It's like in England, where people love to wear old tweed jackets for years and regard a patch of leather behind the elbow as a badge of honor. In French, we call it *le style fatigue*, the tired style.

It was for receptions, during weekends, on holidays, and so on that we got dressed up. It was still the case for my children's generation.

But did you have specific events during the weekend or during holidays that required special clothes?

LA: Church was the only thing. Every year, my mother bought me a dress or suit for church. A hat, white gloves. In photos of me in my church outfits, though, I'm always wearing these clunky oxford shoes! I don't know if I insisted on shoes such as my brothers wore rather than the patent leather Mary Janes that most other girls wore. I do remember hating the little hats, but the Episcopal Church in those days required all females to cover their heads.

FG: In France, you must not look as if you are a fashion follower. Sometimes women like to wear quotations from fashion, the way a writer uses a quotation from another writer. If their shoes are by Saint Laurent or their scarf is by Hermès, that's a quotation. Whatever else they wear is bits and pieces or maybe what they have made themselves.

Frenchwomen make lots of things themselves. Even professional women, if they have some free time or during holidays, enjoy cutting fabric and sewing as a relaxation from the stress of being a lawyer, an executive, a psychiatrist, or whatever.

I myself started sewing when I was about twelve, first learning to cut and to work with a sewing machine from my grandmother's maid, who was very clever and skillful. Then I took a few more lessons with a seamstress who was coming once a week. After that I was on my own.

I had great difficulty fitting things around the shoulder line, so to begin with, I made sleeves that were billowing. Also, when I cut following paper patterns for my size, I had to remember to make the hips a bit narrower and to augment the shoulders. My shoulders were broad because I was a swimmer.

LA: The attitude here is often to wear something so appropriate that you will fit in and not be noticed. Whereas the attitude in France seems to be to make an individualized statement that will make you stand out.

FG: Yes, one is expected to be distinctive. In France,

most people revolve all their lives in the same circles. As a child, you might have some friends who are extremely wealthy and others who have very little, yet you keep the same friends all your life—unless your political opinions become so adverse that friendship becomes impossible. These friendships can be very demanding.

When I go to France, I have to see certain friends, because it would be a great disaster if I did not, even if I'm just there for a week. And right away, they will make a dinner for me, even at the last minute. Everybody in that group will inspect me. So I know I'd better look my best because otherwise it will be discussed.

They will all comment for three months afterward, "Did you see how she looked, poor thing, is she dying?"

Okay, I will attend these dinners, and since I am an artist, I am entitled to come a bit underdressed and a bit more eccentric. They'll expect that of me. So I had better wear something that makes me look both good and unusual. You dress not to show a dress but to show yourself to advantage. To top it all, what I wear should disappear compared with me myself. It should help me look good but not be overwhelming.

So it's not always convenient if I am tired and might not want to make the effort. But in that case, I'd better stay home. And I must be witty too.

LA: When you say that you're sometimes quoting from other fashion statements, that would mean that you're dressing for the women, right? You're dressing for yourself and to express yourself, but you're also dressing for the other women, because they are the ones who can appreciate the quotations?

FG: I have a friend ten years older than I. My grandmother was a friend of her grandmother's. And my children are friends of her daughter's. So it has been going on for four or five generations. She went to the same school as I, so we know a lot about each other, and she is the keeper of my image. That's not always funny, because she has standards.

If I allowed myself to come for lunch without a new haircut or something interesting and bold, she would ask me, "What is the matter with you, are you worried?"

Her husband is also quite a personality in Paris and is very keen about my being distinctive, unusual. Even if this couple is receiving important guests at a dinner, I will always be to his right, because he considers (even now) that I am beautiful and original. So I'd better be at my best.

LA: So the men in France can appreciate the overall look?

FG: Absolutely. He knows as well as she does. He would mostly tell me that it's really a marvelous color for me, blah-blah-blah, whatever thing comes to his mind. We seldom talk about art. I have to be witty, chatty, frivolous, dipping once in a while more meaningfully into world affairs. He will utter flattering nonsense during the whole dinner, the purpose being to relax and drop all worries for a moment.

I will receive more compliments in a week in France than I would receive in a year in the United States. And believe me, it doesn't go any further. It's purely aesthetic; it's not in the least a way to make a pass.

They have a daughter whom I like because she is very intelligent and very much involved in the arts. Unlike her parents, she could not care less about what she wears. But if I'm going to see her, I must dress as well as when I visit her parents, because, even though she doesn't care about her dress, she cares about mine. It would be proof that I am not fond of her if I am not willing to give her aesthetic pleasure.

People in France attach importance not only to clothes but also to objects of everyday life: the plates off which they eat, the cups in which they drink coffee. It's part of the culture, taught early on, so that even a small child should be capable of handling a porcelain teacup without breaking it.

As a child, I thought that those objects were so perfect that they could not have been made by human hand. Even though I could see my mother herself making ceramic vases and plates, it didn't register. To me, porcelain artifacts, so fine and almost translucent, were so perfect that they were like little gods, especially the blue-and-white china teacups. And those little gods I admired were mysterious. I didn't know where they came from and didn't dare to ask, for fear of being told that I was silly.

I thought that they had probably always existed, and yet if someone pushed them to the edge of the table far enough, and farther again, they fell and broke to pieces and had to be thrown away. So these small gods had a precarious existence subject to the skill and care of their devotees, who must do their utmost to ensure their durability.

As I said, my mother was making ceramic objects that she decorated, glazed, and sent to the kiln to be baked. There was an octagonal pot holder she had made that had a little plant arrangement in it. If I stared long enough at the plant arrangement, I began to see a jungle. Stems and leaves became trees; pebbles became boulders. If I stared without blinking, I soon saw a romantic couple walking in that jungle, and I invented their story as I followed their motions through this imaginary paradise.

LA: Those lifelong friends who are the guardians of your image: that's an example of the ways in which the underlying assumptions are sometimes opposite here and in France. Here the assumption would be that as you get to know people, you have to make less effort. You dress up for strangers. I was amused by the idea that you have to dress up for your old friends.

FG: That's part of their love for you. It starts when you're a child. I've thought about it myself, and I realize that it's very strange.

LA: Right, because you hope that old friends know you on a deeper level than just that of your appearance. It's an interesting concept that if you don't dress well for them, it means you don't care for them. They're hurt that you're not willing to make the effort.

FG: You should read Simone de Beauvoir's novel *L'invitée*. The people who are less wealthy are often the guests of people who are more wealthy, for the good reason that the wealthy have country houses. And as a guest, you have to do them honor, and your only recourse is to be elegant, to have chic.

I didn't select on purpose to be mostly with people wealthier than myself. It's simply that many people at my own level of affluence disliked me because my family was too eccentric. But with more affluent people, the more eccentric we were, the better!

In France, it's difficult to go from one social level to another. It can take generations. If you want to rise above your present status in the United States, you might buy a better car. But in France, one way in which you can ameliorate your social fate is by being better dressed. Mr. and Mrs. So-and-so will always be invited to better places because they are so distinguished and elegant.

LA: In other words, if you look the part . . .

FG: You're not yet there, but you're closer. If you're an understudy for a part and the actress gets ill, you'll get the part!

There's a phrase, "Il n'est pas montrable." "You can't show him in public." You can't introduce him to your friends. These are people you're going to see when you're alone. Isn't that awful?

I'm talking about things that are disappearing. Fortunately, I might add. But fashion really does have a social function.

LA: Coming back to the Little Black Dress, I gather the point is not to wear one so that you conform, but rather to combine the items that adorn it in unique ways?

FG: Yes, a Little Black Dress can be worn at the office morning and afternoon. In France, many times people will not leave their offices before 8:00 p.m., and then they will go directly to a dinner. So a woman in such a dress can just change her shoes, give a good brushing to her hair, freshen her lipstick and perfume, change her accessories, maybe adding a long scarf, a vest, or a jacket, some real or costume jewelry to bring a little bit of color, and then she is ready for the evening.

LA: In other words, the Little Black Dress is to fashion what chicken is to cooking!

6. CEREMONIES IN WHITE

FG: The opposite of the Little Black Dress is ceremonial dress, which most of the time in Western countries is white for women—for baptism, for confirmation, for weddings, even for death, since the shroud is white.

LA: In this country, white is also for debutantes.

FG: I did that in black. I didn't have a real debut. Since my mother had been sixteen when World War I began and since there was every sign that World War II was just around the bend, she said I should start going out at fifteen as though I were eighteen because otherwise I would never have that opportunity.

All the other girls had blue or pink gowns, but I decided on black moiré in my own design. I'd seen the film *Jezebel*, in which Bette Davis wore a red dress that looked black in that black-and-white movie, and I thought, "What a good idea."

I started going to parties in this evening dress with young men in white tie and tails. You brought your own "dancer," one young man, or several. So I would arrive with five! I was younger than most of the other girls, and my dancers were about ten years older than I, so the other girls hated me. Usually, my dancers would dance only with me. Otherwise, they talked among themselves and smoked cigarettes and looked bored. Then we left early and finished the evening in a nightclub. My parents liked it, since if I was with five men, they could be sure nothing would happen to me.

LA: Did the men accept the situation, or were they competing with each other over you?

FG: I was a snobbish young girl, and they were snobbish young men. We were all dandies. Dandyism was the essence of it.

LA: They had mistresses on the side?

FG: Sure. We were supposed to go to those parties, but I could end the evening in a jazz club if I wanted. Many times, two of the five would leave us and go see their other women. It was a good excuse for their parents that they were supposedly with me.

All the parents thought that the worst that could happen was that one of them would eventually marry me, and that was thought to be all right. I don't think they knew about the mistresses, and my mouth was sealed. Lots of things were going on in my generation that the previous one didn't know about.

LA: At my debutante party, all the young women wore white strapless Scarlett O'Hara gowns with hoopskirts and kid gloves that came above the elbow. Satin shoes, Merry Widows, the full regalia. There were twelve of us, and we were coached for weeks on how to curtsy, waltz, all that.

It was held at the country club, and we were presented in a spotlight. The couples waltzed in various patterns. Eventually, the fathers cut in and danced with their daughters. The point of it all escaped me then and still does now. It was like a wedding. I guess we were marrying society.

FG: In France, some young women were presented to the court in England. I might have done that except that the war came along. It was part of French Anglomania.

LA: So young Frenchwomen wanted to be presented at the English court, and young Englishwomen wanted to go to Paris to lose their virginity! In the Catholic Church, do you christen babies in white dresses?

FG: Yes. I had a very long christening dress in linen and lace, with a little bonnet. It's the same for boys and girls.

LA: Most of the babies in my extended family were christened in my maternal grandfather's christening gown.

FG: In my father's family, there were three Leclere sisters, famous fashion designers at the time of the empress Eugenia, before 1870. They did embroideries on linen, beautiful lace fans, children's attire, cashmere shawls from India sold in Japanese lacquer cases. One of the sisters was my great-grandmother on my father's side.

When I was four years old, my mother wanted me to be nicely dressed for the wedding of my aunt, my father's younger sister, so my grandmother Gilot gave some of that beautiful handmade lace to decorate a volant dress. With all those layers of lace, I looked like a chick with feathers. I disliked it tremendously. I thought I had never looked so ugly in my life, even though apparently it was absolutely charming and delicious.

I was maid of honor with my cousin Jacques, who was dressed in an Eton suit. We were holding the train of my aunt Mary. Just behind us was the sexton, who was wearing a bicorne hat with ostrich plumes and a blue, red, and gold uniform with short knickers and high white socks and black patent leather shoes with big buckles. He was pounding on the floor behind us with this big silver staff.

My cousin said, "It's dangerous here. Let's leave. He's going to kill us. Let's run for our lives."

I thought my cousin knew everything because he was six months older than I. So I dropped the train. He grabbed me by the hand, and we ran away. It was a great scandal in the church. We didn't run very far, because our parents stopped us and put us back in the procession. We were crying, but they kept assuring us that it wasn't dangerous.

Marcel, Jacques's brother, was five years older than he. That afternoon he said, "I understand why you ran away, because you look so ridiculous in that dress. You look like a chick, not a little girl."

That was awful for my pride because, even though I was only four years old, I was already a little coquette. I said, "Yes, I don't like it, but what can I do?"

He said, "It's very simple. Let's go to the billiard room, and we'll pluck you."

What was said was done. He took one end of the lace and turned me in a circle, ripping the lace off in a spiral.

My mother came looking for me and found me half undone by my cousins, and she was furious. She dragged the three of us in front of the other parents and our grandmother to witness the destruction of yards of this seventy-year-old handmade lace from the Leclere sisters, which was extremely valuable. (My aunt's veil that day was six yards of it.) Until then, we hadn't realized that what we had done was awful. All the adults looked pretty miffed, so I thought things didn't look too good for my cousins and myself. We were questioned in detail because my grandmother wanted to assess our degree of consciousness of what we had done.

Marcel said, "We thought she looked like a chick, and we didn't like her that way, so we had to remove the excess."

Fortunately for us, my grandmother said, "That's what happens when you dress children like little monkeys." (Bang for my mother. Of course she disliked my mother.) She smiled and added, "They are too young to be responsible."

Marcel was her first grandson, and I was her godchild, so she thought we could do no wrong. I thought she was a good sport to take it so well. I had great respect for her. She was really interested in the truth of situations. She didn't smile very much, but she never lost her temper either. She was a person to be reckoned with.

LA: You wanted to be wearing your cousin's Eton suit?

FG: I liked some dresses, but I hated lace above all because that's something that for sure no boy would ever wear. For parties, little boys sometimes wore velvet or silk, so these were fine. But I drew the line at lace. So that was my first catastrophe with a white dress.

LA: In 1991, there was a march on Washington for abortion rights with some 500,000 participants. Antoinette

Françoise at the age of two with her cousins
Marcel and Jacques.

Françoise (second from right) and her
cousins dressed for a family wedding.

Fouque came over from France with a dozen members of the MLF to show support for American feminists.

When you march in these demonstrations, usually you've ridden all night on a bus, you get off and march, then get on the bus again and ride back home. You don't sleep much, and your clothes and hair are a mess. People dress comfortably in jeans and tennis shoes and sweatshirts. But the French delegation wore antique white gowns. It was such a contrast to the American women, who were mostly unwashed and unkempt.

Antoinette gave a speech up on the podium, and the sunlight was backlighting these lovely women all in white, and everyone at the march was stunned. It was like a vision up there on the stage in front of the Lincoln Memorial, with hundreds of thousands of people watching in awed silence.

It seemed symbolic of the suffragist marches in the early twentieth century (in which my great-grandmother had marched), when the women had dressed similarly. One of those marches had been led by a woman in a white gown riding a white horse. It gave the audience a sense of participating in some unstoppable progression, the responsibility for which had been passed along from generation to generation of women. It was very effective, but what struck me most was how theatrical it was.

FG: They were demanding their right to control their own bodies as women. I think it might have been an attempt to show that a woman is in possession of her own body and that that body is pure. Whatever she decides about her own body is for her alone to determine and is to be respected. In colloquial French, abortionists are referred to as *faiseuses d'anges*, angel makers.

I think there's more emphasis among French feminists on the importance of maternity for a woman, too. Nevertheless, there is also an insistence on the right to determine when individual circumstances are appropriate for that. This isn't seen as a contradiction. In American feminism, there has been a tendency to negate women who want to be mothers, yet mothers can also be feminists.

French feminists regard as feminist women who accept their feminine bodies. They are interested in grooming and fashion not in order to be superficial but in order to be women. Whether in their private lives they prefer men or women is a different matter, as is the question of whether they select to be mothers or not. They want equality in their difference, not equality by assimilation to male standards and values. If you lose your femininity in France, you're done for. Since you're not going to gain masculinity in any case, you're just losing whatever power you might have had.

LA: Here, at least in my generation in the sixties and seventies, what you were aiming for was androgyny, developing both sides of your psyche.

FG: But as we've said, in France men are much more feminine, so why should women aim to be more masculine than men?

LA: Frenchmen may be more feminine in terms of their behavior, but they're still masculine in terms of their privilege.

FG: That's true, but mostly politically speaking. In France, there is no segregation of the sexes. You would never have a luncheon that was only women or a dinner that was only men. Whatever your private preferences, you are still in a non-gender-segregated society.

LA: During the years when I was married, I was wearing jeans and sweatshirts most of the time because I didn't want the trouble of trying to look attractive.

FG: Since I'm a painter, I wear jeans most of the day. Picasso used to say I bought things either at Woolworth's or at Hermès. The fact that you wear one doesn't prevent you from wearing the other.

LA: What's interesting, though, is what it says about a woman if she isn't interested in her appearance. My mother wasn't interested, because she was depressed. At a certain point, I wasn't interested, because I didn't want to encourage attention from men.

FG: When men work in white-collar jobs, they have to dress appropriately. If women want those jobs, they have to dress appropriately too. Women in France maintain certain aesthetic standards because they want economic equality. They need to be able to compete in the job market, and appearance is a currency in that situation.

In the United States, women seem to want to have their cake and eat it too, dressing however they want but expecting the respect due to someone who has taken the trouble to look good. In Europe, we've had a much harder life for centuries, so we try to look good in the face of adversity.

Some people avoid these issues because they lack confidence. If they think their face or their body isn't first-class, they may think, "Well, by neglecting myself, I'll appear not to care."

LA: After I went through this phase of jeans and sweat-shirts, I fell in love with a woman. I went out and bought myself a new skirt and cashmere sweater set. Through loving her, I learned to love the feminine in myself.

FG: You reconciled yourself to yourself. That's very important.

LA: Still, what I prefer is androgyny, someone who is comfortable with both the male and the female aspects of herself or himself.

FG: In France, even if you don't want men, you want them to desire you so you can have the pleasure of saying no! Why should you prevent yourself from having such joyful moments?

When I was eleven, the Catholic Church proclaimed 1933 a Holy Year, since Christ had died when he was thirty-three. My maternal grandmother, my mother, a first cousin of my grandmother's who was a deacon, his nephew who was a priest, and I went to Italy on a kind of pilgrimage by train, stopping in Florence and Assisi.

After that, we went to Rome, where we were supposed to be received, along with twenty other French people, by Pius XI, a very nice man, unlike his successor, Pius XII. Pius XI was very democratic and had difficulty dealing with Mussolini, so he was okay.

For an audience with the pope, women are supposed to wear black with black mantillas, and girls are supposed to wear white silk and white lace mantillas. As you know by now, I hate lace. There's a limit to femininity, and lace is it. I like linen, silk, cotton, wool, even embroidery. But lace—no! Lace is too much.

We were staying in a nice hotel, and I went to my room, and what do I see on my bed? A white dress, with a crepe de chine pleated skirt and a top of Irish lace, with a white lace mantilla next to it. So this was what they had concocted for me for that event.

I thought, "Oh no, I'll look too ridiculous."

Next to the bed was a writing table where I had been writing my memoirs of the trip, so I took the bottle of ink . . .

LA: You little brat!

FG: I made a spot on the beautiful pleated skirt, knowing that if I did it on the lace, they'd know I'd done it on purpose.

Then I shouted as if in despair, "Oh, what a terrible thing! I've made a spot on my skirt, and now I can't go to the audience with the pope." Meeting the pope didn't mean much to me at eleven.

My grandmother and my mother arrived from the other room to find me tearing my hair and crying.

They said, "Don't cry. It's only fountain pen ink, and we can have it cleaned for tonight."

By five o'clock, the dress was back in perfect condition. This was a terrible moment for me because I had been taught that the pope was infallible, so I thought he would call me a naughty little girl in front of all those people.

So it wasn't a very happy little girl who saw the Swiss Guards dressed in their uniforms of red and yellow. We waited in a large room with a throne. In comes the pope, all in white. He blesses us and then sits on his throne. He says in French how pleased he is to see us.

Then he says, "You, little girl, come up here, and I will bless you specially."

LA: Like Santa Claus!

FG: I walked up to the throne thinking I was about to be exposed. I knelt and kissed his beautiful white and gold slipper, then kissed his ring. He blessed me and said absolutely nothing about my terrible crime. Apparently, he was infallible in matters much more important.

Strangely enough, my remorse was much more awful afterward because no one had punished me. I knew what I had done was really nasty, yet I had gotten away with it. So you see that ceremonies in white for me are associated with misbehavior on my part for which nothing bad happened.

LA: And always to do with lace.

FG: Yes, I have a very bad relationship with lace.

Early on, I discovered a notion I called distributive justice. In my relationship with the adult world, many times I hadn't done anything bad. But I would get punished because the adults were sure that I had.

I would never humiliate myself to say, "No, I didn't do it, and I don't deserve this punishment." I would be stoic, like an ancient Greek or Roman, and I would say to myself, "This is the punishment for the things I really did that they didn't discover."

I decided that in life punishment and reward usually are not matched. Most of the time, bad deeds go unseen, and good deeds also go unseen. By and large, the saying "No good deed goes unpunished" is true. So you have to be stoic in front of punishment. You say nothing and take your blows when you get them, and you take your praise even when it's not deserved.

LA: It's like my theory that when you scrape the side of your car, rather than getting upset, you should assume that that is the accident you were going to have that day and be thankful that it wasn't more serious.

FG: Exactly true. When I was fifteen and still had some illusions about life, I had a recurring dream in which I was dressed in white for my wedding, riding in the car going to the church with my father.

All of a sudden my memory failed me, and I said, "Father, whom am I supposed to marry? I'm tired this morning from having my hair done and all that, and I just can't remember."

My father said, "I know you like jokes, but this is a bad one. You know very well whom you are marrying."

I thought, "Well, never mind. I'll just turn my head when we get down to the altar and see who it is so I'll know whether or not to say yes."

So when I got there, I looked and saw the body of a young man, but the head was a blank oval.

The church was full of people, the organ was playing, the bridesmaids were processing, everyone was very joyous except me. My anxiety mounted as I stood next to that man with a perfect body and no face. I thought any minute I would see the face appear.

The priest said, "Do you accept this man as your husband?" But he didn't say his name.

So I said, "Please can you tell me who it is I'm supposed to marry?"

Chaos broke out in the church. The chandeliers fell, the choirboys fled in disorder, the guests rushed out. I remained alone in front of the altar, all of a sudden wearing only my white underwear. It was like a de Chirico painting. I had this dream several times.

Just to give you some idea of the anxiety that ceremonies in white provoke in me! I've been married twice since but never in church and never in white.

LA: A southern wedding is indeed like a waking nightmare. Mine started three weeks before the actual day. Richard, my intended, came down from New York. We had seven bridesmaids and seven ushers who arrived from all over the United States. For three weeks, there were breakfasts, luncheons, teas, showers, dinners, cocktail parties, all day every day. It's mainly because all the adults, friends of my parents, wanted to give parties because my parents had given their children parties, or would in the future.

The way you get through this if you're the bride is by drinking. I'd been drinking champagne for three weeks by the time my wedding day arrived. I was pickled. It was like my debutante party: it was all so ingrained in me that I didn't think to question it, even though my bridesmaids from other parts of the country were astonished by this tribal ritual.

On the day of my wedding, we started with champagne at ten in the morning, and the service was at seven that evening. I had my hair done and then went to a buffet in the afternoon, after which we were supposed to get dressed for the service.

All of a sudden I got fed up with the whole thing and dived into the swimming pool with my new hairdo. All the guests gasped with horror because a southern woman can't get married without a bouffant hairdo. I came out

Lisa, dried out after her plunge into the swimming pool, on the afternoon of her wedding in 1966 (the bodice is of Brussels lace).

dripping wet, and the women bundled me into a car and took me home for a mass blow-drying session.

I wore my sister-in-law's dress, which was Brussels lace with a floor-length skirt. Lace again! It was a gorgeous dress. But I was sad because I didn't get to pick a dress of my own. I'd worn my older brother's hand-me-down clothes and played with his cast-off toys throughout my childhood, and now I was wearing his wife's wedding dress. But my parents thought it was ridiculous even to think of spending hundreds of dollars on a new dress when here was this perfectly beautiful one that had been worn only once before.

There was a huge tent in the backyard of my house for the reception, a band, more champagne. Everybody danced, and then Richard and I left for our honeymoon in Portugal.

So I didn't think to question until it was too late whether or not the role of wife was one I could fulfill. Diving into the pool and wrecking my hairdo must have been my feeble gesture toward escape.

FG: That's parallel to my gesture of throwing ink on my dress. All those ceremonies are rites of passage, and it's quite normal that a young person would be reluctant to go from a state already known to a state about which you may have doubts and reservations. Our type of reaction is typical of both you and me as rebellious characters. Most girls are enchanted to put on beautiful dresses and go through those rituals. To the contrary, that's what they want. They aren't dubious at all.

LA: What color did you get married in?

FG: With Pablo I didn't get married at all. Although,

strangely enough, one day before we started living together, he took me to a church in Antibes to make me swear always to love him, and he swore the same thing. But there were no witnesses. We were alone in the church. He had remnants of Roman Catholicism in him, so he had to sanctify that union.

My first husband, Luc Simon, and I had a civil wedding at the city hall in the Fifth Arrondissement. I didn't want a religious wedding, because then there is no divorce! By that time, I was fairly skeptical about the duration of any relationship. I was dressed in pale pink. We had a lunch afterward at an inn by a river outside Paris.

Jonas and I were married at the city hall in Neuilly around noon. My dress was in different colors with geometric patterns, like an ancient Greek fabric. I've always avoided white.

LA: Were you confirmed?

FG: Yes. First Communion, followed by confirmation a year later. And that was in white. But there was no lace; it was pleated linen. It didn't offend me, so I behaved. At that time, I was fairly religious, and that's an important ceremony because it has to do with your faith in a personal way.

LA: We had confirmation in the Episcopal Church too, and I wore a white dress. But the whole thing didn't make much of an impression on me.

Another of my ceremonies in white was Class Day at high school right before graduation. The entire school gathered in the gym, and all the girls were dressed in white. I wore a dress in rayon with knife pleats. The different awards were handed out, and it was announced that I

Françoise, age ten, at her First
Communion.

had been voted Most Intelligent or Most Studious, I don't remember which. But the result was the same: I was mortified. As a southern woman, if you're intelligent, you're supposed to conceal it. The country singer Dolly Parton, well known for her blond bouffant, is a good example. Someone once asked her if she was offended by dumb-blonde jokes, and she replied, "Lord no, because I know I'm not dumb and I know I'm not blond!"

I was second in my class, but no one had noticed until it was announced at Class Day. Plus, I wasn't actually very studious; I just found the work easy. So here before the entire school I was revealed as the most studious girl with the highest marks. Another humiliating ceremony in white!

White is supposed to symbolize innocence and purity, which is why it's used for all these ceremonies of transition from one state to the next. Even shrouds, which were traditionally white, represented the transition from this world to a higher state of being.

But think about the Ku Klux Klan and their white robes and hoods. To me, they represent evil and death. Whereas the Little Black Dress, with its origins in mourning, is often worn to parties and celebrations. So nothing in this life is ever simple!

7. ENGLAND'S GREEN AND PLEASANT LAND

FG: Since I was an only child, I was often very shy at parties until about 6:00 p.m. Then all of a sudden I'd discover that I was enjoying myself and meeting new children, and I'd get all excited. Once I got excited, I got very excited.

LA: What age are we talking about?

FG: From about six to twelve.

LA: Birthday parties?

FG: No, afternoon parties from about 3:00 p.m. until 7:30 p.m. They were called *matinées*. Many times there would be thirty or forty children, all extremely well dressed, and we danced with each other.

LA: At age six? We didn't have anything like this in Tennessee.

FG: Yes. At six, I knew several dances. I had a little boy-friend named Robert, and we danced well together, so we tried to avoid having to dance with children we didn't know.

LA: Ballroom dancing?

FG: Yes. There would be at least two afternoon parties for children each year at my maternal grandmother's house, and I would go to eight or ten parties a year at other children's houses. My grandmother had a large sitting room, so she would have the real Guignol from the Champs-Élysées for maybe an hour.

Sometimes they showed cartoons or home movies. Then tea or chocolate with cakes. After that, the children were supposed to dance and talk together. Sometimes in other people's homes, I knew almost no other children except the one who had invited me. So you're in a corner and you're bored.

Around 6:00 p.m., there would be a farandole when all the children took each other by the hand and wound through the entire house. By then, I had usually found some kindred souls and had begun to laugh and giggle and shout. I'd go from shy to hyperactive. When my parents came to pick me up, I'd have become a firebrand. Also, I knew I had to go back to being alone, so it was harder on me to have to leave.

At home, I had to get back into my everyday clothes and attend dinner that way, before taking a bath and going to bed. My father said I had to reintegrate the "grayness of days"—meaning that a feast is something apart from the normal, so it has to be finished before you end the day. Otherwise, you are still on cloud nine the next day and don't pay attention at school. So you had to resume your normal persona before you went to bed. *Grisaille des jours,* it was called.

Françoise at age seven wearing a party
dress by Decré Sœurs.

LA: Were these bacchanalia held on weekends or school days?

FG: Always on Thursday afternoons, which the children had off from school. During the weekend, families often went away.

LA: I was just thinking about the poor parents whose children weren't invited. The process of exclusion started when the children were six?

FG: I was five when I attended my first one. I was absolutely out of my mind with fear. It was a costume party, on top of it all. I was Little Red Riding Hood. I was furious because I wanted to be disguised as a boy. I felt ridiculous, but my mother and grandmother weren't to be dissuaded. I had a little basket. And of course, the little boys were making fun of me. Fortunately, the dancing started, and that was the time of the Charleston, which I could do quite well. So Little Red Riding Hood was dancing the Charleston. The Charleston and my friend Bob saved the day.

Another time I dressed as Bicot. Bicot and Suzy were our equivalent of the Little Rascals. Bicot is the boy who's too small. With his gang of Ran-Tan-Plan, he makes all kinds of trouble, but he doesn't get caught, because he's so small. He wears a red-and-black-checked cap, an Eton collar, and short pants. That was very pleasant for me because I identified with him.

LA: Maybe he was your alter ego—the bad boy, since you were such a good girl.

FG: Maybe so. I had borrowed the costume from my cousin

Jacques, and I was pleased to be wearing boys' clothes. Gray flannel short trousers.

LA: The only parties we ever had were birthday parties to which you invited ten or twelve neighborhood kids. And when we got to be about eleven, we started having boy-girl parties with dancing and kissing games—Spin the Bottle and Post Office and Five Minutes in Heaven. Each involved going off into some dark room and kissing someone you'd never kiss in the light of day. In junior high school, there were semiformal dances at the country club a couple of times a year.

FG: After the age of twelve in France, you have a lot of schoolwork, so the parties stop. You begin to indulge again around the age of seventeen.

LA: You've talked about the group of children at the house in England where you spent several summers learning English. I love your story about your wearing a turban and silk pajamas. You must have absorbed the stereotype of what it meant to be a Frenchwoman?

FG: Rather, it had a lot to do with American and English movies, which I was crazy about. And since I was supposed to be learning English, I was encouraged to see them. They included all kinds of things that were not typically French, but were rather Hollywood sophistication. In all those American comedies, women like Jean Harlow were dressed in fashions that were absolutely different from the French because they were so exaggerated. At that time in France, everything had to lean toward minimalism.

When I was thirteen, I had a long cigarette holder like Marlene Dietrich's. Smoking didn't interest me that much in France, but in England I liked to pretend I was older than I was to make myself a bit more important.

Also, at twelve in England you are just a child and have to go to your room at 6:00 p.m., whereas in France children go to bed rather late. If you made them go to bed at 6:00 p.m., there would be a revolution. I thought I'd better pretend I was a bit older, so I lowered all my hems to make my skirts longer so I wouldn't look like a child.

LA: Did it work? Did you have to go to bed at 6:00 p.m.?

FG: They let me stay up because they realized a French girl was not used to that. Fortunately for me, there was a British lady staying there who insisted I be her fourth for bridge. My father was a good bridge player and made me play bridge with them when they needed a fourth. I wasn't crazy about bridge, but it was a good excuse not to have to go to bed.

I also bought some tangerine lipstick at Woolworth's and some tweezers to make my eyebrows a thin line like Marlene Dietrich's so that I always looked astonished. These efforts went unrecognized because nobody cared!

My third year there, I was almost fifteen and had started sewing for myself. I had seen Carole Lombard in satin pajamas and a three-quarter-length robe of the same cut. I made the same thing in pale blue satin. The cut was masculine, which I liked, but what could be more feminine than satin? I made a second set in salmon pink.

The house was full of eight or ten young people from six to twenty years old. The boys' rooms were on the third floor, and the girls' on the second. Downstairs was a dining room, a living room, a library, a sitting room, et cetera. In the garden were a cricket court and two tennis courts. On the girls' floor were two or three rooms with two or three beds in each. Every girl had her bed, her dressing table, and an armoire, each in her own corner.

There was a very large bathroom near the staircase leading to the third floor, where the boys stood to watch the girls as they went to take showers. I knew my pajama-and-robe sets were very nice, but there was still the problem of hair, which doesn't look very good when you're coming back from the shower all wet. It spoils the whole effect. So before summer holidays, I went to the Galeries Lafayette in Paris, where I found some beautiful fabric, striped like a rainbow. I used it to make a turban and some scarves. I liked the contrast between the pale satin and the extravagance of my turban.

I put on this outfit to travel down the hallway to the bathroom, and I could glimpse the boys hanging over the railing swallowing their saliva the wrong way. Sometimes I would also have my long cigarette holder and a cigarette at eight o'clock in the morning. They thought I was the quintessential French ingenue, but I thought I was an American sophisticate! The net result was rather positive.

Carole Lombard, Jean Harlow, Marlene Dietrich—those were the three I admired the most.

LA: But they were basing their glamour on an exaggeration of French style. It was all a case of massive cross-cultural misunderstanding!

FG: These actresses always wore robes in satin with something very unseemly like fox fur around the edges. But I thought that was a bit much. I knew where to stop.

The first time I came to that house, the mother, Aunt Jean, told me the rules and said, "You are expected to be down for breakfast at 9:00 a.m. with your room absolutely straight."

Since I was an only child, I never did my room in Paris. So the first morning, I left the disorder, thinking I would do it after breakfast.

But she saw it and said, "You must stay here and do it. I have told you it must be done before breakfast."

She didn't say it in an unpleasant manner. She simply said, "That's when it must be done."

I admired her coolness and restraint so much that I raised my children that way. I told them, "Everything that is not explicitly forbidden is allowed."

I thought that system was more convenient and less complicated than the French one, which is item by item, and you're allowed to do something on Friday but not on Sunday. You never knew where you were. In England, if you gave your word that you wouldn't do something, there was no spying on you.

That's one reason I like Anglo-Saxon countries. Your word is as good as gold. In France, they suspect you all the time and are after you like the police. In England, it's like a contract. You are a free agent within certain limits. If you transgress those limits, you are guilty in front of your own conscience, not in front of another person.

LA: It's like the difference in the legal systems. In England you have to be proven guilty, whereas in France you have to be proven innocent.

FG: Exactly. In France, you're under suspicion all the time, and you end up wanting to do bad things so that the bad prophecy will be fulfilled.

In England, I was encouraged to become responsible for myself. I was respected as a human being even at twelve. They assumed if I gave my word, I would abide by it. Thus, I felt much more bound to do what I said I'd do.

In class, the English students were responsible for their own discipline. In France, when the teacher went out of the room, we made a mess of everything. There was too much restraint, so we exploded all the time.

Someone once wrote, "In France, you can't have evolution; you have to have revolution." Things are so tight there that it becomes unbearable and you explode. In England, there were limits, but they weren't so tight that you wouldn't feel free within them. You had a better opinion of yourself.

When I came back from England, I had become a person. Adults said, "Oh, she's become a snob." But it wasn't that. It was that in England I had acquired self-respect. I wouldn't be disagreeable, but I would indicate if I wasn't of the same opinion. I still did as I was told, but I let it be known if I didn't think a course of action was correct. My parents always said that after England I became a different person, but in fact I just became a person.

LA: From a sinning worm into an individual?

FG: Yes, it was the beginning of my self-respect, which in turn engendered a certain amount of self-confidence. The English encourage reliability, responsibility. Other people respect you because you're a responsible person.

Now I feel much more at ease in Anglo-Saxon countries than in France, where things are always so complicated. There are always mysteries, and you shouldn't say this and you shouldn't say that. Not that the English say much. But they don't because they want to control their emotions, not because they want to create mystery. In France, there is all this Machiavellian diplomacy. You spend all your time complicating life. In England, it was much more straightforward. Here are the rules, and the rules have no exceptions, and the rest is a free-for-all.

I sent my children to the École Alsacienne, a Protestant school in Paris with basically the same guidelines as in England. I think it's better to develop the good side of people. Gertrude Stein once said if an accomplished writer or artist meets a younger writer or artist and spends all the time telling him what's wrong with his work, the younger person will wither.

To the contrary, if you compliment what's good, they understand that this is the way to proceed, and their limitations fall by themselves like deciduous leaves. In France, people spend all their time talking about what is wrong. It's the national sport.

LA: I agree that if you focus on the positive, it will force out the flaws.

FG: In France, if I did something good, the reaction was "Yes, but it could have been better." Or, "Who do you think you are?" Or if it was imaginative, it was criticized for not being rational enough, and vice versa. But nothing is perfect in this world.

The father of that English family was a commodore in the British navy, and his wife who I called Aunt Jean was Scottish. Both were High Church of England. My mother had told me I had to go to the Roman Catholic Church for mass on Sundays.

Aunt Jean told me, "You see that oak there? As far as I'm concerned, you could pray in front of that oak and it would be just as good."

But to please my mother, I rode ten miles on my bicycle to a tiny little Catholic church. The priest was Irish, and I couldn't understand a word he said in English. At confession, he couldn't understand my French accent. We agreed that I would enumerate my sins in Latin. Aunt Jean loved that. She laughed.

She used to say, "Why are you in such a rush to go to heaven? Don't you know it's drafty up there?" She had such a sense of humor about those matters, which was new for me. My mother wasn't strictly orthodox, but she wasn't ironic on such topics.

LA: The best aspect of Protestantism is that it circumvents a priesthood.

FG: You accept the rules because you know they are valid, having consulted your inner conscience. So you don't break them. It's the basis for an ethic that is more possible.

LA: More human in dimension, certainly.

FG: Sure. Something you can actually abide by. After four summers of that, I came back to France beginning to know who I was. People couldn't push me around as much as before. In class, I began challenging received opinions. It made my life much more difficult.

LA: In French terms, you should have pretended to agree and then thought what you wanted in private?

FG: What I learned in England was so much in accordance with my natural bent that I of course adopted it. Later, in 1960 and 1962, I had exhibitions of my paintings in London at the Mayor Gallery. Thanks to my dealer, Fred Mayor, and to some influential trustees of the Tate Gallery, I had the good fortune to rent an artist's studio in Chelsea (the largest and most beautiful I ever had) on Sydney Close, a set of mews near Sydney Street. I felt in a very positive frame of mind, similar to what I had experienced as a teenager spending summer holidays learning English in Aunt Jean's house near Lee-on-the-Solent, where I progressively found my way toward self-reliance and inner balance through the unexpressed trust I felt around me. Never too many words: silence is often the best teacher of an adolescent.

Later, within the large empty expanse of the Chelsea studio, new knowledge suddenly unfurled around me once again. It was like a zoological invasion of animals: hawks, owls, monkeys, lizards, dragonflies, horses, parrots, frogs, even phoenixes, descended into the middle of the Greek ruins I had started to depict on canvases of different sizes, some very large.

In 1942, I had visualized all manner of birds, fish, and crustaceans, pertaining to usual classical animation in Dutch still lifes and "vanities," but hardly any dogs, cats, or horses. But in 1965 in London, it was as if all of a sudden the quintessential dwellers of Noah's Ark had chosen my studio as the place in which to disembark. From one day to the next, without previous visits to the zoo or particular forethought on my part, the different species came at my beck and call.

This sudden ascent to power that could later be used and transformed at will is one of the most astonishing experiences in an artist's life, since usually evolution is slower and results from sustained attention and progressive knowledge.

In 1966, an exhibition of my recent works, mostly rather large canvases, was planned for the Leicester Galleries in London. I informed the director, Mr. Phillips, that the general theme of the show was related to Greek antiq-

Françoise beside a taxidermied albatross shot by her father (1955).

Françoise standing in front of a Greek-related "floating painting."

uity. He seemed slightly alarmed, saying, "You know, we here in England have priority over ancient Greek civilization. Why, otherwise, do we spend so much time at Oxford or Cambridge?"

Rather astonished but not really disturbed, I asked him just to visit my studio and judge if he liked the works, ancient Greece–related or not. After all, I had not defaced the Elgin Marbles! When he came and viewed all those animals frolicking among Greek ruins, he was quite elated, suggesting that my eccentricity certainly would be acceptable in a country where the boundaries between rationality and irrationality were often hidden in the fog.

"After all," he said, "you use the Greek ruins only as sets in which to display the carnival of animals." After a short silence, he added, "In England, we love animals."

I must say that the show was quite well received. It was obvious that my works expressed passion but didn't demonstrate ideological theories, in keeping with the British temperament. This was the reason I had originally fallen in love with the English language. All the eighteenth-century French writers—Montesquieu, Voltaire, et cetera—admired the British, the constitutional monarchy, freedom of conscience.

LA: We had the same thing growing up in the South—an advanced case of Anglophilia. My mother reread Jane Austen every year. In school, even though there's a remarkable southern literary tradition, we studied only the English classics. It was like being in a British colony, in the sense that you felt you were stranded there in the New World and you looked back to England for your roots and values.

FG: English literature has made a great contribution to the world. It has a certain moral, though not moralistic, ethos, which develops that sense of personal responsibility. That was a great gift they offered the world.

LA: Yes, when I was in that little town in Tennessee, my equivalent of your summer school in England was my reading of British literature, especially the women—Jane Austen, the Brontës, George Eliot, Virginia Woolf. And Dickens, Sterne, Fielding, Conrad, Hardy. So I absorbed that value system through the literature. That was my personal church. The Episcopal Church didn't speak to me; it didn't have any relationship to the questions I was asking. But British literature did, and I read those books as though they were my sacred scriptures, looking for answers to questions like what it means to be a decent person and all that.

FG: Even the romantic novels like those of Scott embody the same ethos. Chivalry and generosity. Individualization has something to do with British culture.

LA: I lived in London for two years, from 1978 to 1980. When my daughter, Sara, was nine years old, her father and I decided we wanted to live outside the United States so that we could experience another culture. We picked London because we were Anglophiles but also because then Sara wouldn't have to learn another language for school. Also, I saw London as the crossroads of the world, with people from all over the former empire flowing through it.

Another reason for London was that I had become friends with the writer Doris Lessing and wanted to know her better. Ten years earlier, I had read all her books and written her a fan letter. She wrote me back, and we developed a correspondence that lasted, off and on, for some forty years. Each time I visited London, I would see her, and often when she came to New York as well. She also stayed with us in Vermont several times, enjoying our back-to-the-land lifestyle. I remember her swinging like a little kid from the branch of an old apple tree while we picked apples to press into cider one sunny autumn afternoon.

I had been writing short stories since I was sixteen. But when I read Doris Lessing's novels, I first understood that you didn't have to write about going on the sea in ships, or to war, or into the wilderness. And you didn't have to use fancy symbolism. You could write in plain language about what was going on around you every day—relationships, motherhood, housework. And if you did it well enough, you could end up with a novel. So I wrote two novels that were rejected repeatedly by publishers. My third novel was called *Kinflicks,* and I started submitting it to editors.

I had never told Doris Lessing I was writing, because I didn't want her to think that wanting her help with my writing was why I had become her friend—because it wasn't. But another friend of mine let the cat out of the bag by asking her how she liked my new novel.

She replied, "What? Lisa writes novels?"

She immediately wrote me a letter saying, "For god's sake, send me your manuscript!"

By this time, *Kinflicks* had been accepted by a publisher in Boston. It is structured so that comic chapters alternate with tragic ones, because I thought that was essentially how life works. This publisher said he wanted to publish it on the condition that I remove all the tragic chapters because they were too depressing.

Doris Lessing had by now read *Kinflicks* and liked it, so I asked her if she thought I should remove every other chapter.

She said, "Don't be ridiculous! That would ruin your

Lisa looking out her barn window in Vermont on the publication day of her first novel, *Kinflicks*.

novel. Let me give it to my editor and ask him if he thinks you should remove those chapters."

So she gave it to Bob Gottlieb at Knopf, and he said that not only should I not remove every other chapter, I should let him publish it as it was.

Doris Lessing gave me a wonderful blurb for the jacket, and *Kinflicks* went on to become a *New York Times* best seller. It was also translated into sixteen other languages. So I now had a writing career and enough money for a stay in London.

My then husband, Richard, and I rented a flat on a side street right next to Hampstead Heath. Sara attended the local primary school for one year and a private day school for the second year. On many Sundays, Doris Lessing hosted a lunch at her apartment that was like a British version of a salon. The other guests were writers, editors, painters, translators, journalists, businessmen, computer geniuses, shopkeepers, professors. Some lived in London, but many were just passing through from all over the world. Doris was a superb cook and produced great vats of stew and giant roasts, huge bowls of English trifle.

She was short but solid, with her graying hair pulled back into a bun. Her eyes were quite intense when she turned them on you. She wasn't particularly interested in her wardrobe, and her apartment was cluttered with stacks of books and papers. During the years I knew her, she lived first in Maida Vale, then in Kilburn, then in West Hampstead in a tall, narrow row house. She preferred not to talk about her own writing, though she loved to discuss other people's, and she liked nothing better than wry jokes and anecdotes. We used to take long rambles across Hampstead Heath, discussing everything under the sun.

Through Doris Lessing I met Idries Shah. Born in

India to a Scottish mother and a father from a noble Afghan family, he lived in Tunbridge Wells. He was said to be the spokesperson for contemporary Sufism. Many people define Sufism as the mystical branch of Islam. But Sufis themselves claim that their methods of spiritual teaching are much more ancient than Islam, Islam being just the latest in a long line of belief systems that have harbored and protected Sufism down through the ages.

Idries Shah had adapted many Sufi classics and teaching stories for contemporary readers. I read them all and, for the first time, encountered material that put to rest my anxious search for meaning on this delightful and terrifying planet. He often invited those interested in his work to his estate. His guests would sometimes do a bit of gardening or cooking, and after dinner Shah would talk—for two minutes or two hours—rarely about anything religious or spiritual, often in anecdotes from daily life. He was probably the funniest person I've ever known. Yet I often came away from these talks with a fresh grasp of what it means to be a human being.

So, like you, it was in England that I finally began to grow up, both creatively and spiritually, even though I was already thirty-four years old.

Yet I ended up wanting to leave England and return to Vermont. I encountered so much anti-Americanism, and I couldn't see the point of living in a place in which I was despised for being who I was.

And if I wasn't being despised, I was being seen as an exception: "Well, you're okay, but most Americans are awful."

Also, I was involved with a woman who lived in the East End, and I spent a lot of time out there. So I saw firsthand that horrible British class system at work and also the racism, the Pakistani bashing and all that. British literature had inspired me from childhood, and two British colonials, Doris Lessing and Idries Shah, had helped me become an adult. But the reality of England and the English didn't live up to my expectations. Did you encounter a lot of anti-French stuff?

FG: Oh yes. The British are not great Francophiles.

LA: Some can be very insular. England is, after all, just a small island.

FG: When an English person referred to a French novel, he'd mean a dirty novel. French novels may be immoral, but writers like Stendhal are very important. To debase them is as despicable as any other type of bigotry. I didn't discuss that when I was there, because I thought that French literature is very complex, and unless you've been brought up in that culture, maybe it's inaccessible.

Also, most French novels are about adultery, and in England adultery is considered a very bad thing, even if everyone is doing it. Woman isn't divinized as in France. Everyone in England is supposed to do his duty, and adultery isn't on the list. In France, adultery is considered the result of passion, so even if it's often disastrous, it happens.

When they wanted to wrangle with me about that, I just said, "Look, you don't even read French, so you're in no position to judge."

LA: English novels always end with marriage, whereas French novels always begin after marriage.

FG: In France, what is of interest is what happens when you transgress. If you want to summarize the French novel, essentially it's always *Tristan and Isolde.* You have all the elements of the intrusion of the irrational, fate, magic.

Tristan is supposed to find a bride for his uncle King Mark. When he meets Isolde, her nurse has put that philter in a crystal jug so that whoever drinks it will fall in love with whoever else drinks it. During the trip at sea, Tristan and Isolde drink it by mistake and fall in love with each other. They are going to transgress, but they are not guilty.

LA: That's very Catholic!

FG: Yes, an accident of fate removes responsibility. A well-meaning servant has concocted that potion so that the young woman will fall in love with the old king, but unfortunately the wrong people drink it.

When Isolde at last meets King Mark, she's already in love with Tristan. They didn't do it on purpose, so it's a transgression, but an innocent one brought about by chance. Their love has to be expressed, and they become lovers, which brings about their own destruction. But all this happens without anyone being responsible or guilty. That's so French! Terrible things happen, but it's no one's fault.

Whereas in England they want you to become responsible. So you become a teetotaler, and you don't drink any potion when you don't know what it is. Just a nice cup of tea.

LA: The only English novel I can think of in that pattern is *Wuthering Heights.*

FG: It's true that Heathcliff and Cathy are blinded by their passions, but in a sense they're responsible for what happens to them, because why did Cathy choose to marry someone else? There is no deus ex machina to make them transgress without their being aware of it. Aha, nuance.

A drama is something where very evil things happen, but it is just psychology, the confrontation of malevolent and innocent characters in given circumstances of time and place. It's not fate, not unavoidable destiny. *Wuthering Heights* is a drama. Shakespeare wrote dramas. Racine wrote tragedies. The Greeks wrote tragedies.

Is it Oedipus's fault that he goes to bed with his mother? No, since he doesn't know she's his mother, so he's tragically guilty but not dramatically guilty. In France, you are never responsible for the bad things you do, whereas in England you had better be.

LA: That's also true in the Catholic Church, because even if you sin, you go confess it and are absolved.

FG: Exactly. "Où le péché a abondé, la grâce a surabondé." "Where the sin was abundant, grace was superabundant." Whereas in England the attitude is "Please, know what you're doing if you're going to do it."

LA: So that's what makes Shakespeare's serious plays dramas rather than tragedies: individuals make choices that lead to their own destruction—rather than bungling their way, in all innocence, into disastrous situations?

FG: In tragedy, a kind of divine fate falls on characters. They are just puppets in the grasp of cosmic, divine, or demonic forces.

LA: Or as the comedian Flip Wilson used to say, "The devil made me do it."

8. THE MIDDLE PATH

LA: You said previously that your confirmation into the Catholic Church was meaningful for you?

FG: Yes, the ritual sentence is "Je renonce à Satan, à ses pompes et à ses œuvres, et je m'attache à Jésus-Christ pour toujours." Satan is the prince of this world, so you renounce—almost like the Hindus—all the external things to do with appearances, and you attach yourself to the being behind appearances. I was very moved by that idea. I was pondering it for weeks ahead of time. It was a kind of inner crisis for me.

LA: I was not moved by my confirmation. The Episcopal Church is so unemotional. It uses very beautiful language, especially the old prayer book, which I'm sure helped me learn to write. But Episcopalians pride themselves on being cool, particularly in the South because it's in contrast to the various primitive Baptist sects with their rolling in the aisles and speaking in tongues.

FG: There is no external show of emotion in Catholicism, but it activates an inner fire.

LA: The Catholic Church strikes me as highly emotional—the incense, robes, music.

FG: It's aesthetic, but I wouldn't call it emotional. It's highly ritualized, so it's very cool. The Catholic Church doesn't want exaggeration. Adolescent girls especially tend to become high-strung about developing an inner life, so the church tries to damp that down.

LA: I went through all the rituals of the Episcopal Church on automatic pilot. They didn't touch the inner me—not the confirmation, not Communion. I just did what I thought I was supposed to do.

FG: For me, it was important for my inner life. What was demanded of us was that we really mean what we said. But I never spoke about it to the other girls, many of whom were much more pious than I.

LA: Around my house, everything was so authoritarian that the way I coped was to do what I was supposed to without engaging with it. I remember when I was thirteen saying that I didn't want to go to church anymore because I didn't believe in God, meaning the Episcopal god.

My mother said, "You're only thirteen years old. What do you know about anything?"

I thought, "All right, I'll go to church to keep the peace, but I'll think my own thoughts."

But that's what I did about everything. Until I started writing books and telling all the world what I really thought about everything!

FG: Everyone was Catholic in my family, but my mother or my grandmother would say, "We don't necessarily agree with everything the priests say, but you don't have to say anything about it. Those matters are private. Attend church, listen, and form your own convictions."

As long as I had a tutor at home, I was also taught Greek mythology, Arab tales, and Oriental thought. My father was interested in Buddhism. My maternal grandmother was interested in Theosophy. So I absorbed a certain relativism and also a great appetite for metaphysical questions. Religion seemed to me something that belonged to you as much as you to it. You picked what you needed. I never felt it as something external. Or rather, when I felt it was external, as at school, I would, like you, just go through the motions and keep my thoughts to myself.

Maybe in France it's more artistic, with the singing, the stained-glass windows, the frescoes. Mozart, Vivaldi, marvelous music during the services. It was not emotional, it was artistic. We were encouraged to follow the aesthetic path, to seek God through beauty. That's very Catholic.

In France, you didn't ask yourself, "Why am I Catholic?" because at that time almost everyone was Catholic. You don't think it's extraordinary to have a nose, because everyone has one.

At the same time, the French, who are very individualistic, obeyed the church only when they wanted to. The church in France was much less tyrannical than in other places, not like in Spain, where you really had to do what they said. In France, you just said yes, yes, yes and did no, no, no without thinking very much about it because you saw everyone else doing just the same. People didn't have very many children, so they were obviously using contraceptives, which were forbidden. People would recut the dress of religion to their size and desires.

During World War II, when we were defeated, we saw that Pope Pius XII was in fact on the side of the Nazis, and

Inner Chambers, Françoise Gilot, 1994, black ink and washes, 23⅝" x 17¾"

that was really too much. That is what cut the umbilical cord. That's when I stopped going to church. Until then, even if I had had my doubts, I observed because it was a part of being French. But then we were defeated, and some priests were preaching that we were defeated because we deserved it. I thought the Germans were no more deserving to win than we were to lose. This was absurd. Marshal Pétain, a Catholic, said we must repent. What is this? Please. No, we are not going to repent, and we are not going to obey.

That was the break, because it was clear that the church was being political, which it wasn't supposed to be. Of course quite a number of priests were in the Resistance, but basically all the bishops, archbishops, and the pope were on the wrong side. And after the war, I never wanted to come back because of their attitude about birth control, abortion, all that. Nowadays, half the French people who were practicing Catholics are no longer so. People have had it with a religion that always puts you in the wrong and asks from people things that are meaningless.

LA: In Tennessee, there was always the feeling of being embattled by the Baptists.

FG: In the United States, there are so many different sects. If you belong to one, you have to be serious about it because it's so small an entity. This is different from a situation in which you have 50 million people professing to believe the same thing and adapting it to their own purposes.

You also have 50 million Catholics, but that's out of 300 million people. One-sixth, as opposed to France, where almost everyone used to be Catholic. In Italy, too, everyone is Catholic and interprets it as he or she likes.

LA: In Tennessee, there was a tiny Catholic population and a handful of Jews and Episcopalians, up against a vast majority of Baptists, Methodists, and Presbyterians of every stripe.

FG: Then each has to affirm himself or herself loudly so as to be heard and to abide by the rules of that specific sect, as opposed to adapting a general creed to your own purposes.

Since Pope John XXIII, the church has lost most of its aesthetic trappings, so lots of my friends don't practice anymore because it isn't appealing. If you loved the service in Latin, why would you want to hear it in French with a poor text?

LA: That was the only thing the Episcopal Church had going for it, in my view, the beautiful language of the prayer book. Then they modernized it. It lost its mystery and became like watching television.

FG: There was a French bishop named Lefebvre who wanted to keep the old Latin rituals, but that didn't work either, because he was reactionary. Probably in this new era, with all the telecommunications, the needs of people are quite different. Church was important at a time when people would meet only once a week. During the third millennium, all the new modes of communication will, in turn, probably become sacralized, and religious aspiration will find another way of being expressed.

LA: It will have to, because the dynamic has really gone out of the organized religions. It's become a question of real estate and hierarchies.

I was amazed when I first discovered Eastern spiritual

teachings. They were so different in quality from those of the Episcopal Church, which had nothing to do with the questions I was asking myself about the purpose of my life.

FG: All the scientific discoveries of the twentieth century—the relativity of time and space, the curvature of space, et cetera—are much more in agreement with the Indian Vedantas, even though they are so old. Of course it's more appealing to us than a message that doesn't relate to what we are experiencing in the present.

LA: It's odd, isn't it, that some of those ancient scriptures have maintained their ability to provoke questions and answer them in a way that organized Western religion hasn't?

FG: Eastern religion is much more purely metaphysical and philosophical. Also, there is no dogma.

LA: So it can't be superseded or disputed, as Christian dogma has been repeatedly.

FG: The Eastern way of thinking about the cosmos and the atman of the universe is so different from all the trappings of Christianity. One can believe in the Bible in a symbolic way, but to take it literally, as the fundamentalists do, is absurd.

The notion that the world was made in seven days is just a metaphor. Taken that way, it is beautiful and interesting. "Et la lumière fut"—"Let there be light"—is marvelous poetry. I'm all for that, but let's not take it to be like turning on the electricity.

LA: Almost from the beginning, Protestantism split into

all these sects with minor points of difference. My grand-mother's uncle was a Baptist preacher famous in southwest Virginia—John Calvin Swindall. He was the head of the Soft-Shell Baptists and spent his entire career fighting against the Hard-Shell Baptists. The only difference was that the Soft Shells believed anyone had the potential to be saved. The Hard Shells believed, first of all, that only Baptists could be saved and, second, that there was pre-destination. Whereas Soft Shells were into salvation by works. They had horrible battles for decades in that part of the country over those issues, which to me seem irrelevant to the need for individuals to find meaning for their lives.

FG: There are no wars worse than religious wars. Look at the Muslims and Hindus in India. When India was sepa-rated into Pakistan and India, the Muslims in India head-ing for Pakistan met on the road the Hindus in Pakistan heading for India, and millions were killed.

Or look at France in the sixteenth and seventeenth centuries. *Les guerres de religion.* Whenever one side was winning, they killed everyone on the other side, and vice versa.

LA: That's still going on today between Hindus and Mus-lims, and among the various branches of Islam in the Middle East—as well as with the Islamist terrorist attacks against Western targets and the retaliatory attacks of Western troops, mostly from Christian backgrounds. But in my opinion, none of these groups are authentic spiri-tual entities, whatever they may believe about themselves. If they were, they wouldn't behave like this. One of my favorite Middle Eastern sayings is "Learn to behave from those who cannot."

Cultures evolve, so formats for spiritual teachings

Falcon's Abode, Françoise Gilot, 1993,
black-and-white ink, 20" x 26"

have to be updated to stay abreast of the shifting psychic makeup of the students, even though what is being taught may remain constant. Formats that worked in the past have to be abandoned, like outgrown shells. Unfortunately, many people cling to those shells, sometimes fashioning them into weapons with which to bash those clinging to other shells.

The whirling dervishes of Turkey are a good example. The poet Rumi, who was also a Sufi teacher, said that his students were so lazy that he instructed them to stand up and start whirling, just to get them on their feet and in motion. He never intended for this whirling to petrify into a "spiritual exercise" for use outside his school in thirteenth-century Konya.

So those claiming to represent a particular religious tradition often don't—any more than those who bomb abortion clinics in this country under the banner of Christianity are actually Christians. The world is littered with counterfeit groups from which any spiritual dynamic has departed and with adherents who don't even realize that they are frauds. They're like the cargo cultists of Melanesia, who, observing that supplies for Westerners arrived in airplanes, built airplanes of straw and shortwave radios of coconuts and then waited for supplies to arrive from the sky.

Which isn't to say that the real thing doesn't also exist.

But previously you said that the ultimate goal of French culture is (or was?) "to take the givens of the world and perfect them, abstract them until they almost attain perfection."

FG: To define them and refine them. The refinement is the work of the soul on itself, so to speak, the effort of the psyche to better itself. To aim at beauty is to continue creation.

Even the most Catholic of our writers, Paul Claudel, in that famous play of his, *L'annonce faite à Marie*, shows physical beauty as a metaphor to express the purity of the soul. At the beginning, it's springtime during the Middle Ages, at the time of the cathedrals.

Pierre de Craon, the master builder, beholds his fiancée strolling among the trees in bloom, and he says something like, "Salut, oh toi, ma fiancée, parmi les arbres en fleurs."

So he expresses a desire to rejoice in the beauty of creation and not be sad all the time, to be one with the springtime of life.

All the same, the soul also has to accept the tragedy of life. I can't remember exactly what happens in Claudel's play, but that marvelous girl, Violaine, gets leprosy. So she who was so beautiful is tried through the leprosy of her body, yet her soul becomes more and more pure.

This is just to say that the Catholic attitude is that the world of appearances is not to be condemned. It can be appreciated aesthetically, but that's a first level. And maybe if we can experience that first level, we can infer that there are higher levels. But we must not refuse to see that first level, the visible one.

LA: Well, not only do they not refuse to see it, but the Catholic Church actually uses the senses in their rituals, with the incense, chimes, choirs, robes, which make it profoundly sensuous.

FG: And the beautiful architecture, the music, et cetera. Catholics believe that it's through the senses that they can reach the spiritual part of human beings, exactly like in

India. In India, they tell you that there are nine gates to the body: two eyes, two ears, the mouth, the nose, and down there. They think that a spiritual experience is homologous to a sensuous experience, not the same, but homologous at a transcendent level.

In the biblical poem Song of Songs or in some of the most beautiful writings of Saint Teresa of Avila, the ecstasy of the mystic in union with God is expressed in the same vocabulary as the ecstasy of the senses. And the snake of spiritual energy called Kundalini is first coiled at the base of the spine, and then it rises through the different chakras to the crown of the head.

LA: Well, that makes sense to me. But in France I've often heard sexuality defined pejoratively as an animal act that has to be transcended. I consider myself an animal, a human animal. But I love animals, in some cases more than people! So I don't mind regarding myself as one. Which isn't to say that there aren't other aspects to me.

FG: Well, it's just an inner contradiction. Pascal said a long time ago, "L'homme n'est ni ange ni bête et qui veut faire l'ange fait la bête." "Man is neither angel nor beast, and who wants to play the angel soon plays the beast."

Most French people think that eroticism is an art or that it should be an art. Therefore, all the imaginative complications that people bring to lovemaking are welcome—and certainly not akin to the instinctual behavior of beasts in heat. It is fathomlessly more complex, and it can take place at any point in the year! Whereas when animals mate, it's at a certain season, and it's just for procreation.

LA: Yes, but why should it have to be an art to be significant? Why couldn't it be just an animal act that's pleasurable? A meal doesn't have to be haute cuisine to be delicious and nourishing.

FG: Intercourse without love—lust or the desire to seduce, to conquer, or to succumb—is an animal act. Nothing wrong with that, but after one goes through the experience a certain number of times, repetition occurs. It gets so boring that you want to try different possibilities. It's nice to jump into bed, but if you have to rehash the same motions again and again, pleasure is replaced by tedium.

LA: Yes, but it seems as though the need to turn everything into an art is a way of expressing dissatisfaction with the thing in and of itself.

FG: Well, because the physical possibilities, even if varied, are limited. Yes, leave the world as it is, and it tends toward entropy. Everything has to be refined, ameliorated. That's culture. It's an alchemy. It is true that in France, we wish to transform what exists in the raw and initiate a process of evolution, leading perhaps to more perfection, aiming toward an ultimate enlightenment.

LA: It makes for a very admirable culture. I'm just trying to get at the differences. And I think, in a sense, that's different from the Eastern attitude that doesn't have to turn everything into an art, that accepts the world as it is.

FG: No. *They don't accept it at all.* That is a different viewpoint.

LA: Well, the Sufis say that the apparent is the bridge to the real, which is basically the same thing you were just saying about Catholicism. That the material world is a metaphor for, and a pathway to, higher things.

FG: I don't know Islam that well, but I can tell you that in Indian Hinduism the objective reality of this world is entirely negated. What appears to our senses is supposed to be an illusion, the realm of relativity, so it's refused.

Whereas I would call the French attitude much more comparable to that of the Chinese. For the Chinese, the world, and I mean the world of the senses, is what we want to treat as real because what we can perceive with our senses is also what can be processed by our brains, our minds.

In China, as in France, the best possible way toward intelligent action is what is called the middle path. The middle path is the path that takes the extremes into account but thinks that virtue stands in the middle. Nothing in excess, said the ancient Greeks, and even the Romans stated the same concept: *In medio stat virtus.* Human beings have to know about the extremes but should always revert to the line in the middle, which is the narrow path of rectitude.

To achieve balance, it's necessary to refine all the elements, which can coexist in a chaotic fashion, and to incorporate however much of each fragment can be made to integrate into an organic whole. There is no culture above the Chinese one, and the Chinese think that the French are the closest to them in terms of their approach to life.

LA: I'm not trying to rank cultures. I'm just trying to understand the differences among them.

FG: No, I think it's neither good nor bad. In France,

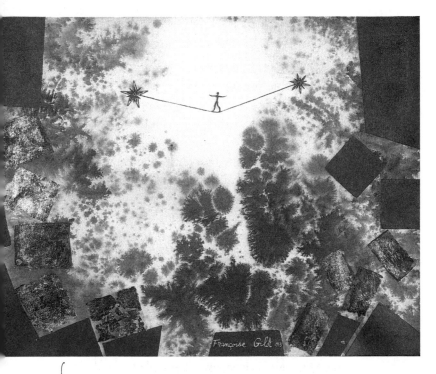

Star Walk, Françoise Gilot, 1993, black-and-white
ink and gold leaf, 20" x 26"

people feel that less is better. They strive toward serenity. Less is more there, whereas in other cultures *more* is more. "Less" implies a choice; "more" implies the absence of control, the storm and the fury. Chaos is a natural condition; order is a choice.

Still, you cannot protect yourself from the storm and the fury. Otherwise, you are a bigot of some kind. So you have to take cognizance of the storm and the fury, and then be strong enough, like a good smith, to bend the extreme parts of the circle and bring them back together. Then you have a certain amount of dynamic tension. You have to bring things back into balance, because if you stay at the stage of the storm and the fury, you stagnate.

The American photographer Mapplethorpe wanted to witness all the extremes. But even he couldn't stay there, because in order to live a little bit longer, or to be a bit more knowledgeable, he photographed flowers instead of dramatic erotic subjects, so he was coming back to the implicit rather than the explicit (because, after all, flowers are sexual organs too).

It's well and good to pretend that you are extreme and are going to remain extremely extreme, but one doesn't. Either one dies, or one has to come back toward the middle, following the usual trajectory of a pendular movement.

It's hypocritical, too, to say that a person has a complete, unfaltering oneness of purpose at all times in life. If people are not sometimes contradicted by their own opposites, they are either inhuman or artificial. And finally, such an attitude becomes hypocritical.

LA: I think my culture of origin, Appalachian culture, would say that all is *not* chaos, that underneath the seeming chaos is a pattern, and that our job as human beings is to drop the illusion that we can control anything at all, so as to open ourselves up to an intuition of the harmony, unity, and purpose that have always existed beneath chaotic surface appearances.

But this is a belief system that is bred into children who grow up in small towns and country settings. We watch the seasons cycle, we watch the crops sprout and grow and get harvested, we watch the animals mate and give birth and die. Any chaos is usually the result of human or natural violence that intrudes out of the blue, wreaks havoc, and recedes, until the next eruption. Nature restores her own order without our interference.

And the reality is that historically no culture has fared any better than any other. Look at the Chinese, who not so long ago decimated twenty million of their own people during Mao's Cultural Revolution. Every culture is brutal, each in its own way. In France, the Catholics slaughtered the Huguenots and, earlier, the Cathars.

Of course, an individual may manage to transcend the constraints of his or her specific culture. But what is interesting to me is the particular mix in each culture of the intellect, the emotions, the spirit, the will, the five senses, and how each culture brings them together in a slightly different brew. It is really quite fascinating.

The French say, along with Descartes, "I think, therefore I am." Americans would probably say, along with Frank Sinatra, "To dream the impossible dream." But I do think the French recipe works very well. It's an admirable culture.

FG: Well, it has been on the make for two thousand years, and it's similar to Chinese culture except that the latter has endured for more than five thousand years! The type of culture aiming at balance and wisdom started with the Chinese and is then to be found in the ideals of the ancient Greeks. France might be the last exemplar of culture, in the best meaning of the word. It may take another form in a different place in the future.

If life is symbolized in squares of black and white, as on the chessboard, the path of the initiate is at the limit between black and white, walking the thin line between black and white, never completely in the dark, never completely in the light, living at the edge of both extremes. But that narrow path in the middle is just a line, difficult to tread without straying.

LA: It seems to me both you and I in our work are trying to integrate and balance the light and the dark. But in this country, people mostly want the dark. For instance, Mapplethorpe's sadomasochistic photographs get much more attention than his flowers. And then there's the obsession in popular culture with vampires and zombies and serial killers. The French seem to like the dark, too, *les films noirs* and all that. But the people who want to find a balance between the two are fairly few.

FG: Many people perceive the dark spots as stronger, more profound, as far as art is concerned. Supposedly, going to the bottom of a well is more profound than climbing to the top of the Eiffel Tower, which seems to me a bit silly.

I had a cousin about four years older than myself who was studying philosophy under Jean-Paul Sartre at the Lycée Pasteur, a public school in Neuilly, the residential suburb where we all lived.

Jean-Paul Sartre kept telling them, "Ah! You are superficial; you are the children of the bourgeoisie. You are self-satisfied; you never try to get to the bottom of things."

My cousin, who liked a bit of mischief, asked him, "We are supposed to go to the depths, are we not?"

"Yes, of course, you must go to the depths," Sartre replied.

So the next week, my cousin and his friends explored the sewers of Neuilly, because obviously meeting the rats and seeing the dirty water and the garbage would enable them to form an opinion about the underbelly of the local bourgcoisie.

Of course, this little excursion became known, and I remember my paternal grandmother, altogether outraged, exclaiming, "What is this? No one ever went to visit the sewers of Neuilly! What a terrible thing that their teacher of philosophy asked them to go deeper beyond ordinary appearances and that their answer was to visit the sewers!"

Of course, they meant that excursion as a joke on two counts, against Sartre and also against some outmoded family principles. But the parents and grandparents were quite offended, imagining the lack of dignity of that scene.

My cousin, who had a good sense of humor, later said, "Well, what about the sewers of Neuilly? When we went into the depths, into the underbelly of the bourgeoisie, what did we see that was so shocking? There were no crocodiles, no dead bodies. All we saw were rats, like in all other sewers."

This farce can be considered a typically French attitude in response to a philosophical question. Transforming a question about self-awareness and sociological inquiry by pretending to understand it literally and making it into a joke is a typically ironic answer to a serious question. And that's why many people think that the French are just superficial and frivolous.

Yet those students won a double victory. They showed their professor that they could be daredevils if they wanted, and their action stirred their parents and exposed their pomposity. The point was made, but it was handled

Celtic Legends, Françoise Gilot, 2013, graphite,
11¼" x 15½"

with irony. People who are heavy in their thinking cannot empathize with the light touch of such a witty prank. It was just a joke, but it was purposeful and revealing.

Once I was in Washington at the Corcoran museum attending a roundtable discussion with the sculptor George Segal, the curator, and myself apropos of Matisse. George Segal stated that for him Picasso was a greater artist than Matisse because Picasso had gotten into the drama of our time with *Guernica*.

I answered that as far as I was concerned, a powerful expression of joy like *The Dance* is just as hard to achieve. My intention was not to diminish the value of expressing drama as Picasso had done. But it's not any easier to express and transmit joy in a metaphysical sense. It's exactly as elusive as it must be to dive into gloom and drama. Both are just as difficult to reach with strength. So I said that if the strength of expression is equal, then the quality of artistic achievement is the same.

LA: Well, to me, the challenge is to integrate the two, to bring them together, because each is true in its own realm.

FG: Yes, I think that as we live in the twenty-first century, we would be well-advised to consider that both have to be there, opposed and complementary. It's a stereotype in painting to say that because of the law of sharp contrast, where the light is greater, the darkness is darker. Of course. If you have just a dim light, you don't have much contrast. If you have an intense light, you have great shadows as well. That's the law of contrast. We can perceive things only in opposition, so we have to maintain the two, and doing only one is not very interesting.

If your vision of the world is pink and blue, it's a little bit silly. And if you perceive everything in black on black, well, what more can you add? The contraries, by opposing each other, define and establish each other. And you can experience the same where gender is concerned. The feminine is necessary to the masculine, and vice versa. The perfect being would be androgynous.

Whatever the prevalent philosophical attitudes that have come down to us as legacies from all the different cultures of the past, each age needs to reformulate them. The times are always changing, so if we have studied some philosophical systems and gone through spiritual experiences, our duty is to express these things in a way that will be appropriate for people in the present and the future. I think that is the real mission of anybody who wants to be an artist.

Acknowledgments

With much gratitude to the following people:

Martha Kaplan, for her help in shaping the final manuscript and finding it a happy home at Nan A. Talese/Doubleday—and for her sound advice always;

Nan Talese, for her intuitive response to our project and her skillful guidance and encouragement in producing the book;

Dan Meyer, for his efficient and cheerful coordination of the many details involved in the publishing process;

Aurelia Engel, for her assistance with the illustrations;

Sydney Goldstein, for inviting us to present this project in its early stages at City Arts & Lectures in San Francisco;

Ina Danko and Mary Jane Salk, for their early readings and enthusiastic support.

Thanks also to the following people at Nan A. Talese/ Doubleday, without whose talents this book wouldn't exist: Maria Carella, who designed the book; Ingrid Sterner, who copyedited it; Emily Mahon, who designed the jacket; Bette Alexander, our production editor; Michael Goldsmith, our publicist; and Lauren Weber, our marketer.

A NOTE ABOUT THE AUTHORS

LISA ALTHER was born in 1944 in Tennessee. She is widely known for her first novel, *Kinflicks* (1975), a feminist coming-of-age narrative that broke new ground in terms of what could be written and talked about. She is the author of seven additional works of fiction, a memoir, and a narrative history of the Hatfield-McCoy feud. Her books have been published in seventeen languages and have appeared on best-seller lists worldwide.

FRANÇOISE GILOT was born in 1921 in Paris. She was a part of the emerging School of Paris. In 1943, she met Pablo Picasso, an artist forty years her senior, with whom she had a decade-long relationship. In 1964, Gilot published *Life with Picasso*, which sold over a million copies in its first year and has been translated into more than a dozen languages. She is also the author of *Matisse and Picasso* and other books. She married the French painter Luc Simon and, later, the American vaccine pioneer Jonas Salk. Gilot is included in the collections of the Metropolitan Museum of Art in New York, the Musée Picasso in Antibes, the Tel Aviv Museum of Art in Israel, the National Museum of Women in the Arts in Washington, D.C., and the Bibliothèque Nationale and Musée d'Art Moderne in Paris, among others. She was made chevalier and then officer in the Légion d'honneur.